MW00513225

About the Author

Chinny George is a trained marketer from the IPE Business School, Paris. She is a trained bilingual office manager from the Alliance Française d'Accra and a trained fashion designer from BlueCrest University College, Accra.

She runs a hair business as well as a fashion styling and wardrobe consultancy business in her country of residence, Accra in Ghana.

Her enthusiasm about mending broken relationships and helping people navigate rocky relationships through the years has inspired the writing of this book.

She loves reading, engaging in creative arts, cooking and dancing.

Chinny intends to continue writing for a really long time.

Ladies and Gents

Chinny George

Ladies and Gents

Olympia Publishers
London

www.olympiapublishers.com
OLYMPIA PAPERBACK EDITION

Copyright © Chinny George 2021

The right of Chinny George to be identified as author of
this work has been asserted in accordance with sections 77 and 78 of
the Copyright, Designs and Patents Act 1988.

All Rights Reserved

No reproduction, copy or transmission of this publication
may be made without written permission.
No paragraph of this publication may be reproduced,
copied or transmitted save with the written permission of the publisher,
or in accordance with the provisions
of the Copyright Act 1956 (as amended).

Any person who commits any unauthorised act in relation to
this publication may be liable to criminal
prosecution and civil claims for damage.

A CIP catalogue record for this title is
available from the British Library.

ISBN: 978-1-80074-133-1

First Published in 2021

Olympia Publishers
Tallis House
2 Tallis Street
London
EC4Y 0AB

Printed in Great Britain

Dedication

I wish to dedicate this book to God. He gave me: the inspiration, the words, an awesome publishing house, a fantastic support system and amazing readers.

INTRODUCTION

Do you remember your first relationship? You had no idea what you were doing or what it all meant, right? Do you still remember how it all made you feel? So giddy with excitement yet so dreamy? You felt like you never should be made to wake up from such a wonderful dream but things happened and it didn't quite go the way you had hoped.

Then came a number of other relationships, each with their different style and lessons, leaving you with more and more questions unanswered. Some people got lucky and figured it out on their own with each experience but most weren't so lucky. How did it get so messed up, you surely asked? Why did you constantly get it wrong, you wondered? Was it just you or did people exaggerate the whole love thing? You were determined to find out.

I'm sure some of you have reminisced about past experiences and how sweet some of them were and I sincerely apologise to those who had bitter experiences which I have reminded you of with my writing but it was a necessary exercise, to enable you hopefully to see things a little clearer as we journey through this book.

Whatever became messed up in your relationship history, was born in the very first relationship you ever had. You were young and extremely naïve. You had no idea what you were doing like I mentioned earlier. That first relationship was very crucial even though you were young because you got to have a first time experience with the opposite sex; seeing life through their eyes. Your personality came alive at this point because you got to discover how strong or weak you truly were and how much willpower you possessed. Traits which would determine the kind of life choices you made later on and how each partner that came into your life would see and treat you. Sounds all twisted and complicated, right? Yet when you think about it, it makes sense as well.

There have been a million books written, a million documentaries watched and a million relationship coaches talking about it but there is only one person who understands how you truly feel or what you have gone through and that is YOU. No two relationships are identical. Everyone has their story and journey.

There may be guidelines but there are no instruction manuals anywhere on how to describe the feeling when you suspect you are falling in love (forget the butterflies in the stomach concept because at some point they fly away) or the pain when you have been hit by the worst betrayal (true knockout punch); it's simply an individual journey and that is one truth we should seriously embrace.

Now, it is important to note that: I am not a relationship coach, I am not writing this based on any reference from books or Wikipedia definitions, nor did I Google any of these things I offer you. Too many of those types of books exist already. This is based on my opinions, my observations, my little experience and the experiences of others. If you do not agree with me, then please don't continue reading because it may stress you out for no reason and I would hate to contribute to your rising blood pressure. However, if you decide to continue reading, know that I have my readers' best interests at heart and hopefully this will go a long way in helping you in one way or another.

CHAPTER ONE
BEING SINGLE

The pressure on young people these days to get married or to be in meaningful relationships with good prospects is quite alarming and can drive anyone at the receiving end completely nuts. Parents are quite bothered that their children are doing well in other aspects of life except in getting serious about finding a husband or wife. I might even add that the mothers are more concerned than the fathers, mostly because of their hunger for cute grandbabies. I understand their craving because babies born these days are really adorable!

The young men and women in question are bothered by three things: (1) they fear they are disappointing their parents, (2) society is putting them through torture by reminding them in one way or the other that they need to be quick about it and (3) they can't figure out how exactly to go about finding who to marry, especially in our present age when too many of the rules which could have made this process easier in the past, have radically changed.

It has become a huge problem and has pushed a lot of people into making hasty and harmful decisions: some people have ended up in violent marriages, some have incurred some huge debts in the bid to have weddings, some have gone into depression because they can no longer take the pressure.

Good news! It doesn't have to be this way! Being single is not a terminal disease. It doesn't mean your life has spiralled out of control. It doesn't mean you have to do all it takes to find someone to latch on to in desperation. It definitely doesn't mean you should stop being happy and being you.

Do you have any idea how beautiful/handsome you are? Do you know how many people are in awe of your intelligence and great personality? Do you know how many lives you touch on a daily basis in the most remarkable way? Why on earth do you let something like a relationship status redefine you?

God has never and will never make mistakes, I hope you agree with me. He took His time to create you and He sent you with an instruction manual to 'go and multiply': Genesis 1:28 and Genesis 2:24 for your perusal. Do you think He didn't put someone here on earth as well, to carry out those instructions with you? Let me remind you that our father in heaven is a master matchmaker because He knows all his creatures and the plans that He has for them.

While you are trying to digest those facts, look up Ecclesiastes 3:1-8. That pretty much sums it up. My dear, there is no delay with God. He works within His timeline and ours is to do something as simple as trust and obey. Have you never heard many stories where people say, 'just when I had given up and had actually stopped searching, I met my husband/wife'? You have been sorted out already. Allow your good shepherd to lead you and there will be no room for regrets.

There is one vital fact that most single ladies and gentlemen ignore. The waiting period is your opportunity to re-evaluate yourself and life choices. You say you are ready to be hooked to another person for life or to share another person's life; how prepared are you? It is not a one-month vacation with someone (oh no), we are talking for life or at least for the long haul. Some people can't even stand their own company but want to drag another person into the equation. Find your groove. Ask friends to give you their true opinions on your personality and use that as a guideline to changing what needs to be changed. (You may lose a few friends for a little while if you don't like what they have to say about you but, okay).

My sister, you say you don't know how to cook, is this not the time to enroll in a cooking class? My dear brother who cannot keep a room tidy to save his life; take this time to acquire organisational skills. What's your plan in this twenty-first century: leave it all to the woman? There is a lot to do, instead of brooding over how many curses have been placed on you by wicked relatives. Every new trait you pick up during this hiatus will eventually prove useful in your relationship when you start one and will change your marriage game when the time comes.

You are single! You need a man/woman to call your own! We have heard and understand you but what kind of man/woman are you looking for? It is either they have no idea or they come up with the most outrageous checklist one has ever seen or heard of. This is the time to be realistic. Do me a favour and throw that piece of paper you wrote the checklist on into a fire or tear it up. At this point, as a grown man/woman, you know yourself and what you can handle. Use that to describe the kind of man/woman you truly believe will fit in and who will be able to tolerate some of your excesses.

Now, let's be real. The 'dark' days will come. The loneliness is like living in another type of hell. You see pictures of seemingly happy couples everywhere you turn. You wonder when all your fantasies will become a reality. You can't stand that friend of yours who just won't shut up about how happy she is. You fear to pick up calls from family and relatives because you can almost bet that they will bring up your pathetic, single life. You hardly attend events anymore because everyone you know is either there with their husband/wife or their partner. I understand exactly how you feel.

The one thing you will not do is to let it bring you down. You will not become a recluse who won't leave the house (your potential suitor/woman doesn't know your house address remember!). Get up and have some fun. Enjoy every bit of it. Whatever you do; I beg you to pray ceaselessly because only God has the key and you need Him.

CHAPTER TWO
FALLING IN LOVE

Have you watched Hindi movies? Watched romantic comedies? Read romance novels? If your answer to any or all of these questions is 'no', pray tell me, on what planet have you been living and where do you get your ideas on love from? I'm not saying these should be your primary sources but we who have done all of the above, will gladly tell you that we learnt a lot.

Let's go back to the Hindi movies, shall we! Sometimes, they are unrealistic but for someone who watched and still watches a ton of them, I can tell you that there is something magical about the way a guy looks at a girl he is in love with and how the girl shyly responds with stars in her eyes. Even if you don't understand the language or don't have access to subtitles, you will feel the chemistry oozing out of your screen in some of those movies (kudos to Bollywood).

There is a little truth to all the beautiful storylines in movies and wonderful details in the books but in real life, it takes a lot more than that to know you are falling in love with someone.

One might say there is no relationship without both parties being in love but it doesn't always happen that way. Some relationships start off on just liking someone or being really close friends for a while, before love happens. There is no laid down system anywhere so don't go missing out on a good thing because you did not fall in love first.

Like I mentioned earlier, it is an individual journey so the fact that Esther and Paul fell head-over-heels in love when they first met, doesn't mean it will happen in the exact same way with Martin and Keira. Appreciate your own journey because it's unique.

How do you know you are falling in love with someone? Here are the basics which I'm sure you have heard before: firstly, you can't stop thinking about this person no matter how hard you try (just not possible). He/she is the first person you think about when you wake up and the last person on your mind as you drift to sleep. You can't fake this one my dear, it's a natural thing.

Secondly, you find yourself worrying about this person's wellbeing more than anyone else's, including your own. You want to be sure they are safe, happy and well taken care of. You can't stop yourself from always wanting to call to check up on them, just to be sure.

Thirdly, the strong urge to be around this person all the time (trust me, if it wasn't romantic, it would be a little creepy). You just love basking in the presence of your love interest. Everything they do around you is fascinating and looks like a wonder, even when you have seen it before.

Fourthly, you are real around this person. No pretense, no lies, no deceit whatsoever and it is made easier by the fact that your love interest accepts you just the way you are.

How do you know you are in love according to my own experience? You just know. It has a way of turning your life upside down. You stop reasoning like a normal person. It changes your sleep pattern. You don't eat like you used to because you are busy thinking about this person and smiling about something which may never make sense to another person. You don't even like other people because they are all interfering in your time, to either daydream about this person or actually be with the person. Anybody who makes the catastrophic mistake of telling you he/she is not right for you, should get ready for the war of their lives. Trust me, it hits you really hard and until you experience what I just described and more, my dear, you haven't fallen in love.

I always joke that falling in love should be listed as one of the wonders of the world because it is phenomenal. Imagine one thing which has the ability to bring out other abilities you never knew you had. You go about feeling like one of Marvel's superheroes because this amazing person is either in your life or about to enter it.

I knew a young lady who used to be so scared to go out at night because she hated the dark. Fast forward to when she fell in love with this young man against her family's wish and you know family: they always have your best interests at heart. Of course, she was defiant. The same person who feared the dark would use a ladder to climb over the fence surrounding their house just to sneak out to meet the young man. Tell me that is not phenomenal. Alas, their love story didn't last forever after but they have remained close friends to this day.

There is a reason it's called falling in love and that is because the force of the fall is something renowned physicists would never be able to explain. It has nothing to do with the physical. Yes, you became attracted to the person but that attraction is fleeting. Within a short time, you get really irritated when the person's true nature shows through. The same things you noticed at first which were so flashy and dazzling, turn around to look ugly and disgusting because that wasn't love.

You fall in love with a person's soul (the true essence of the person), which is why you can: accept the person for who they are, you can overlook their flaws and tolerate their excesses, you defend their weaknesses, you praise their strengths, you uplift them when they are at their worst, you are ready to fight the world when they are under attack, you can't bear to see them in any kind of pain, you laugh at their jokes whether funny or not, you can't be cruel to this person because you feel the pain more and you find ways to make up after a fight. That is how to know you have fallen in love.

Unfortunately, people have downplayed all of these and turned the tables and these days, we see more of lust than love. Everyone should experience this magical feeling at least once. You haven't really lived until you do.

CHAPTER THREE
COMPATIBILTY

You are excited! You think you have found the love of your life! All of that is just fabulous but don't make the mistake many people make. Don't go too deep without hitting the pause button and asking yourself if the two of you are truly meant for each other or asking an even better question: are you compatible?

Yes, I know there is no meter to measure how compatible you are or are not; however, there are natural tools which God put in every one of us, to enable us to determine just how far the love journey would take you and how quickly you need to turn the lights out and say goodbye.

It's quite simple yet overlooked, dear reader... really quite simple. All you need are your five senses and a dose of intuition. You need to be extremely observant because every minute detail counts.

Let's begin with the sense of **sight**. You have heard it a number of times that 'love is blind' but I'm glad to inform you that it recovered its sight a long time ago. People just chose to continue with that lie and it has wreaked a lot of havoc. Look, you have just met this person; you are two very different individuals who have grown up in very different backgrounds. You are in love and we have already established that fact but please watch out for visible signs or red flags, which will enable you determine if you can share your life and feelings with this person.

The last thing I want for you is a broken heart or pain of any sort but you need to be realistic. I am a promoter of love but a huge fan of wisdom as well. It is always better to nip something harmful in the bud before it gets out of control. That is the reason we have too many failed relationships, too many violent attacks and loss of life these days; people are too blind to see the visible signs.

Look out for how he/she treats you when you are together. Look out for how they treat other people who live where they live, at work, their friends and strangers, of course. Look out for what makes you feel irritated, unsafe, disrespected and disinterested. Some might argue that these feelings will not show up in the early stages but I beg to differ. There is something called human nature and it doesn't hide. One way or another, something about this person will pop up. You just have to be vigilant enough to see it.

One more important factor many people overlook is that when someone appears squeaky clean, there is a high tendency that they are truly not. There is no perfect person and the fact that he/she has checked out on all the items on your checklist, leaves room for your internal antenna to be on high alert. You want to bet that the real person will show up in no time? Don't worry, we are not gambling here but you need to be careful.

Let's check out the sense of **hearing** as a tool, shall we! This one hits hard, dear reader and that's simply because it will leave you in a dilemma between accepting whatever you have heard or shrugging it off and moving on with your love-struck life. Let me not run ahead of myself, so listen; there is a high tendency that you will hear stuff about your love interest at the early stage of your relationship. Especially if you are able to meet the important people in his/her life at this stage. You will hear great things and they will make you smile with pride but you will hear the not-so-great things as well.

True, we live in a society where people have a hard time minding their business and there exists some very proud haters but two, three or more different people won't be lying about the same thing at the same time. Listen! You may not like it but listen! Heck, it may not be true but still listen! Don't just go on a crazy campaign against all those who are against your happiness but take what they are saying into consideration; if it's something you can live with then you have nothing to lose, otherwise, please give yourself the needed advice.

Now, the sense of **smell**: you will never imagine how important a person's hygiene is until it hits you in a very unpleasant way. You are crazy in love; so that weird smell you have been perceiving since you met this person has to be something else because when you see this person, your mind tells you, you smell roses. Lies! One day, when you are deep into the relationship, the roses will wither and die and then it will hit you like a tsunami. Make sure it is something which can be fixed from the beginning, with love, of course and that your love interest is the type who won't throw daggers at you for trying. This is very important because you will be spending a lot of time with this person and you don't want it to be an issue.

Next, we check out the sense of **touch**. How does the person react to the way he/she is touched and how do you respond to the person's touch? Some people have never mastered the art of being gentle and some are too sensitive. You may have met a rape victim who is gradually coming to terms with finally opening up to someone else; now, the way she responds to you will be different. Or you meet a young man who is the touchy-feely type. It's his nature to want to hold your hand or hug you at every chance he's got but you don't like that, because your preference is a 'once in a while' thing. There may be a big problem if not handled properly in the beginning, so these are things to be checked. Be sure that some of these factors are things you will be able to handle in the long-run or things you can comfortably live with if they don't change.

Finally, the sense of **taste**. I mentioned earlier that this is an unconventional book and sometimes words would be used in different contexts and this is one of those cases. Taste here is not about how much an individual savours certain flavours and spices. No, it has to do with how compatible we are in our choices of food and beverages. We are different people but if I can't stand the things you eat or drink, it is going to be a huge problem. Trust me, issues like these actually exist. People differ and our diversity is what makes life much more interesting but what looks like it could be handled easily in the early stages of your relationship, may not be as easy as time goes on and changes take place. Let's take the classic case of a strict vegetarian and a non-vegetarian or an alcoholic and someone who can't finish a glass of wine. How easily do you think they can make choices about where to go on dates or which events to attend together? I rest my case.

Earlier on, I mentioned you will need a dose of intuition, right? I stand by this very strongly. Intuition is a unique gift from God which was given to everybody. However, women got a little extra dose (no offence guys) but we don't listen to it as much as we are supposed to. You know that nagging feeling which you swiftly brush away because you don't like what it is telling you? Well, you better start paying attention to it. That is your warning sign and it is never wrong. It will let you know that something isn't right or that you should pay attention to a particular detail; do yourself a favour; please do not ignore it.

So, you have checked all of these facts and you find nothing you can't handle, then congratulations because you have passed a big test on your journey. If you find out after all that it is not worth your stress and this person is not a match anyway, no worries. It may or may not hurt a little bit to let go but when you find that right person, you will be glad you didn't make a mistake.

CHAPTER FOUR
DECLARE YOUR MANIFESTO

I always joke that relationships have reached a point these days where we need to start using contracts to enter them. If you want a two week fling, then sign and we know after two weeks everyone goes their way but if we want to continue, we renew the contract. I am definitely kidding but that might just work.

No one is being honest about what they really want. Boy has his weird ideas about what relationships truly mean and girl has her deluded fantasies about what she is hoping will happen to her in the course of her love journey. Somehow, no one gets the results they expected more than half the time and it is killing relationships more and more every day.

I truly believe that the one thing which will help relationships flourish in our present day, is if true intentions are declared in the beginning. Young man, the lady is not in your head to know that you actually like her but you are not ready for a long-term relationship. It will be very difficult to fit that into any conversation, I know but the amount of pain it will avoid when she is made aware, is worth spilling the beans in the beginning.

Young lady, you know you have commitment issues. The thought of sticking to one person for a long time is a huge phobia for you and yes, people like that exist. It may be psychological and here; on our beautiful continent, it will be considered a spiritual case. Whatever the case, you know the problem exists and it is not your fault. Be honest about it from the beginning and if the man likes or loves you enough to help you navigate those uncertain waters, so be it.

Have you taken time out to scrutinise life and the many issues we face on a daily basis and as we grow older? Don't you want to avoid as many of these issues as possible, if you can? You can start by stating your agenda from the beginning.

A man would meet some promising and happy, young lady who has a lot of potential and a bright future: find a way into her life, deceive her into believing he is in it for the long haul, she gets really comfortable and chases away another man who had better intentions for her, he squanders seven years of her life, then gets up one day to tell her he is getting married to a girl his family chose for him, which is a lie because he actually met her a month ago. The young lady gets mad and decides to get him back for what he has done. She ends up hurting him and destroying herself in the process.

All of that drama could have been easily avoided if the man had told this young lady that he just wanted some casual fling. He knew from the beginning that it had no future but he was enjoying the freebies he was getting and using her to while away time until he found 'his missing rib'.

There exists another set of people who are just unbelievable. He/she has managed to be truthful to you from the beginning (there are some really honest people in the world): you sat down there listening attentively to him/her baring their soul to you, you know for a fact that you cannot handle everything they just told you, yet you are nodding your head like an agama lizard, tomorrow you get up and say 'I can't take this anymore'. What exactly is wrong with you?

He/she might be fascinating at first. I know, after all, that's why you fell for this person to begin with but please look beyond that and save yourselves a world of unnecessary issues, by declaring your true manifesto early enough.

CHAPTER FIVE
JOB DESCRIPTION

Anna and Jeff met at a pub through mutual friends. They immediately fell under each other's spell and began a relationship which was the topic of discussion within their circle of friends. Anna would go to Jeff's house to wash, clean and cook to the extent of missing client deadlines in her consultancy business. She became so invested, that she would try to dictate who Jeff associates with, where and when he is allowed to hang out and if he dared defy her, she would go into a nagging rage. Jeff became very frustrated because he loved Anna a lot but he didn't know for how long he could take the 'suffocation' he felt in the relationship.

Andy and Maria had been seeing each other for just three weeks when he started hounding her phone with calls to come to do the washing for him, to attend family events or to cater for his friends. She didn't understand the demands because she felt things were going at a ridiculously alarming rate and she needed the pause button before she exploded.

The two scenarios above are very common these days and if you say you have neither seen nor heard of something like these, then I would really be amazed. What I can't stop wondering about is how we got it so wrong as a generation. I know I can be a bit old-school sometimes but what is wrong with that? After all, everything we have now has its foundation in the old-school, so why can't we refer to that era since it is obvious things worked out better for us then than they do now?

A quick reminder of how things were done back then: a man saw a young lady he was very much interested in, he either made his intentions known to her or he made them known to her family, she gives her consent if she is interested, a courtship which is heavily chaperoned begins, they get to know each other better and wedding preparations begin soon after.

The new generation decided to add some 'flavour' to the mix: guy meets girl and asks her out on a date, girl accepts, date happens and intentions are made known, a relationship is born, girl spends time in guy's house more than in her own, girl becomes pseudo-wife to guy, guy milks the cow free for five years, girl nags guy to take things to the next level, guy gets angry with her nagging and cheats on her, girl is heartbroken and breaks up with guy.

I get it! You want to show your man how much you care about him, so you go about making sure where he lives is neat and tidy. You want to make sure he is eating well so why not just make the meals yourself. Who wants an unkempt boyfriend with stains on his shirt? So, you decide to do his laundry. He will most likely be lonely so I will pack a little bag and go to stay in his house. All that is quite commendable and you are a lady with a golden heart (I'm being sarcastic).

The day you met him, was he not well dressed and tidy? Did he look underfed in any way? Did he say, "Please, I have a condition where I get awfully lonely and I need someone to be with me so I don't get a panic attack."? You and I know the answer to all of the above is NO. Why then have you decided to turn yourself into a wife/nanny? The annoying part is that somewhere in between, you lose yourself completely. To what end?

He walked up to you because he found you fascinating and

loved your personality, he wanted to get to know the beautiful lady with the charming smile, he loved listening to your scintillating conversations.

Allow men to ask before you run ahead of yourself to offer unwanted services. Just calm down and enjoy the relationship. If you must cook, then let it be on request or a once in a while thing; which you will agree is quite reasonable. You can visit as much as possible but reduce the sleepovers to the barest minimum. If he wants a permanent bedmate, then he should put a ring on it. Stop jumping one level to get to the other; where exactly are you running to and who is chasing you? Stop showing desperation and your lack of self-worth in the name of showing love.

To the men, I have this to say: if you want a girlfriend, stick to having a girlfriend and if you want a wife, do the needful. Don't sit there and clear the plate of food she served you when all the while you know she is wasting her time and doing way too much. You might think you are enjoying the free perks but the repercussions when things come crashing down are really not worth those pots of soup.

Let's try and be reasonable. Build meaningful relationships and friendships. Get to know and appreciate each other deeply. You are allowed to take it up a notch when/if you get engaged. Then you can exhibit some wifely potential so the man has a feel of what he will be getting and vice versa. You will be amazed at how much more you value each other and how much you discover about yourselves and life in general.

CHAPTER SIX
WHERE DOES LOVE LIVE?

A friend complained to me a while back that he had never had any luck in the love department because he kept meeting girls who broke his heart and caused him a lot of pain. He went ahead to ask where people find love. I listened to him pour out his heart and felt sorry for him because his despair was visible.

He is not the only person facing this uncertainty of where to start looking for the one who will make life more meaningful and somewhat sweeter. Too many people go through life without truly finding love and that is so sad. Some find it in the most unusual places after they have searched for what would seem like ages and many more are still swimming in the vast ocean of incertitude with no proper directions.

The truth is that love has no permanent address. There is no map anywhere which will magically link you to the person you were destined to meet, so please change that mindset if you have been living with it. Finding love has nothing to do with 'where' but everything to do with 'whom'.

Every one of us as long as we can remember, has had a checklist with items describing in detail, every quality (both reasonable and unreasonable) we would like our partners to possess. In my case, that checklist kept undergoing upgrades after each break up and I threw the list away at some point. You really do need a checklist though, because, just like everything in life, you need something to guide you and to be a reminder to enable you to avoid unnecessary mistakes in future.

I will give you the same answer I gave my concerned friend; take time out to really evaluate. You know yourself and your capabilities, you know what you can and cannot tolerate, you know your likes and dislikes and you know your strengths and weaknesses; so use all of that to determine the qualities you hope to find in a partner. Bearing in mind, of course, that this person should be able to handle everything you bring to the table and vice versa.

After all of that mental exercise, it will be extremely clear where to start looking for the kind of man/woman you have described in your new checklist. You see, it's not rocket science but quite simple and rewarding if you do things right.

I have heard people say if you want the good men or women, go to church. That truly amuses me, because anyone gullible enough to believe that is not ripe yet. The church is not a reliable location to get good people mind you, because the church is a mixture of really good people and wolves in sheep's clothing.

Anyway, you can find love in the bank, church, mosque, restaurant, pub, club, school, market, hospital, prison, cinema, park. It is everywhere and anywhere but there is one key which guarantees the success of your quest and that is to have an **open mind**.

The problem we face nowadays is that society has come up with its own standards for determining who an ideal partner should be. What the person should look like, how successful the person should be, how the same society is supposed to accept or reject them. I don't know how or when it happened but people have allowed these, so-called, standards to overcloud their sense of reasoning and better judgement. The most frustrating part is that the same people who are living by these standards are the same people crying and complaining and it leaves me perplexed.

The level of materialism and flashiness we are unfortunate to live with in our confused generation, is the root cause of these problems. Most of our young ladies just want flash and already made. I agree totally with you that things are hard and you wouldn't want to be hooked to someone who wouldn't guarantee a little breathing space from the poverty and hardship you have been subjected to. Comfort is everything and I will be the last to debate that point but you don't want to be with someone who turns you into a punching bag after giving you a pair of 'red bottoms' do you? You don't want to be with someone who devalues you because he picked you up and polished you to the point that he/she thinks you have reached. It is truly not worth your tears. The bitter truth is that there are more rich frogs than there are true princes and you have done a good job of kissing many of them 'til now.

Keeping an open mind simply means you should expect your dream man not to particularly come in the package you wished or fantasised about. He may not drive up in a Bentley but may be standing close to you at a bus station. He may not have gone to school but he is a hard worker who is ready to give you all he has. Just bear in mind that true happiness doesn't come with a price tag. It comes in the simplest packages so don't be fixated on the wrong ideas and thoughts.

Who says you can't be a hard worker as well? You are educated and young; so build on your own dreams little by little and when you climb that ladder of success and still hope to hook up with your billionaire prince, your success will open more doors for you to meet the rich and famous and he might just be waiting for you there. Let's be wise, shall we!

To my brothers, yours is a different story. I know it is said that men are moved by what they see but you have taken it to a whole new level. Unfortunately for you, God is the creator of everything in heaven, on Earth and under the Earth and it is not in your hands. You have become so shallow-minded that it's downright pathetic. Women come in different shapes and sizes and you have been seeing the one who is clearly meant for you but because she is dark and not light-skinned, overweight and not skinny, she's a flat 'NO'.

You have been running after the light-skinned, slim sister for a long time and she hasn't given you the time of day; then you start making noise about how miserable you are and can't find love. Love has been staring you in the face every day. Let your mind be open to the fact that: she may not have the figure you want, she may not know how to dress properly, her communication skills may be zero, she may embarrass you sometimes with her social handicap but she is the only woman who can give you the right dosage of love that you are looking for and the kind of relationship you crave.

My dear reader, I can't emphasise enough; love is everywhere. You pass it by on your way to work. You opened the door to it when it rang your doorbell. You bought an item from it at the market. Accept it the way you see it and turn that 'lemon you have been given into extra-chilled lemonade'.

CHAPTER SEVEN
LET US PRAY

This chapter is one that is extremely dear to my heart and one I looked forward to writing. Well, slightly more than the others and I will tell you why but first let's go biblical…

1 Thessalonians 5:16-18 says, '*rejoice always, pray without ceasing, give thanks in all circumstances; for this is the will of God in Christ Jesus for you.*'

Psalm 102:17 says, '*He regards the prayer of the destitute and does not despise their prayer.*'

Philippians 4:6 says, '*do not be anxious for anything, but in everything by prayer and supplication with thanksgiving let your requests be made known to God.*'

Jeremiah 29:12 says, '*then you will call upon me and come and pray to me, and I will hear you.*'

Matthew 6:6 says, '*but when you pray, go into your room and shut the door and pray to your Father who is in secret and your Father who sees in secret will reward you.*'

Mark 11:24 says, '*therefore I tell you, whatever you ask in prayer, believe that you have received it, and it will be yours.*'

That is a lot to take at once I know; especially for those people who cannot remember the last time they held a Bible. This was very necessary though, to make my points sink in better.

We live in a world where there are too many distractions and if you are not careful, you will indeed fall off the wagon or go astray. Whether we agree or not, two facts are true; there is good and there is evil. The important point to note is that evil cannot be fought with blows and punches but by the only weapon we have been graciously given and that is, prayer.

We need to take our relationship with God extremely seriously. What kind of life do you truly have without God in it anyway? All your waywardness and carnality, what good exactly did it do? Some of us have not yet been exposed to what it truly means to be a child of God and I would want to personally take you on that journey but since I don't have a personal link to you, I would like for you to reach out to any good church around you and talk to someone and you won't regret it.

In the relationship aspect, I would certainly tell you that you will get it a hundred per cent wrong without God's help. I have tested and proven this remarkable fact.

God created you and everyone else on earth, right? God knows each one of us more than we would ever know ourselves, doesn't He? God is the only one who knows who would be best for you and when, where, how you would meet this person, isn't He? God is the one who will make sure that the relationship flourishes to the level it's supposed to get to, right? So where do you come off thinking you can do all that on your own?

There are some people who have actually acknowledged the fact that God is the only one they need but they do not have faith that He will actually come through for them, so they wait a little and then they can't take it anymore. Looks like God is too busy with other matters and so we quickly move into the world and start making a plethora of mistakes.

Have you ever heard the saying that the best things come to those who wait? It is true. You need to back your ceaseless prayers with a good dose of faith. Trust God completely and you will see your dreams come true in mind-blowing ways.

Most times, when you are not paying attention or obsessing

about it is when he/she walks into your life. I say that with all conviction because it happened to me. I really had stopped paying attention and had channeled all my energy into other ventures. I believed with my whole heart that there was someone out there for me and I trusted God so much, that I knew in His time, He would make it happen. He didn't disappoint, of course. The most amazing man walked into my life and it felt like God had just moulded him especially for me, from my checklist.

Another mistake a lot of us make is that we stop praying when we feel we have had our prayers answered. Big mistake! That is when you intensify because the devil doesn't want you to be happy. The devil hates that love exists and so he will do just about anything to stop it. That is when you see unnecessary issues coming up, there are cases of infidelity and a lot of misunderstandings. You need to pray and commit you, your partner and your relationship to the only one who truly has your back: God.

Brethren, we need to be careful because we live in very dangerous times. You don't need lessons in karate or taekwondo to fight the devil because your battle is not physical. Besides, you won't see him coming and he will thrash you first, (just saying). Your battle is spiritual and has one weapon which is prayer. Don't stop and don't get tired. Your victory is just around the corner and it will be worth the wait.

CHAPTER EIGHT
AGE AND RELATIONSHIPS

I cannot count how many articles I have come across and how many conversations I have been a part of, where age in relationships has been discussed. It has always been an issue but it has become more so in recent times, however, I'm not here to give you a lesson on statistics so let's dive right in.

Back in the day, it was so common to see older men date and marry younger women. The younger ladies were readily called 'gold diggers' because no one could really understand what other attraction there could be except for the material gains. The general response to it was a few cold stares, some comments and a lot of gossip and it ended there. After all, it's a man's world, so we have to take it the way we see it.

These days, there is a new trend; the older women are dating and marrying younger men and it is on a rapid increase. This is actually the bone of contention as many believe it is more normal and preferable for an older man to date a younger partner than a woman doing the same thing.

Let me outline the reasons a man will date younger and vice versa. Some men just live their lives, working and acquiring as much wealth as they possibly can and they dedicate a great part of their lives to doing that. Somewhere along the line, they wake up to the realisation that they are getting old and have not really lived.

Now, according to them, the women their age don't quite have what they are looking for so they look towards the younger ones who are more vibrant, interesting and full of life.

Then, we have the old 'Casanovas'. Those ones are just die-hard philanderers and age has only made it worse. They just believe in having a shiny, new, young girl in their arms every now and then; plus, there's money to spend on them so it's a win-win.

Next, we have the widowers and divorcees; those ones have either been locked up in their grief or in unhappy marriages for a very long time. They feel it is their moment to splurge and they go into the game, big time; after all, they have a lot of catching up to do and who better to show them exactly what they have been missing but a young beautiful woman?

Let's flip to the other side now, shall we? The reasons why a woman dates younger people are a bit similar but more emotional. It is common knowledge that women are very emotional creatures. They are on the look-out for that one person who satisfies most of their emotional needs and most times, they don't care in what package the person comes.

There are those, like their male counterparts, who were so engrossed in chasing dreams and building careers that at some point, it finally hit them that they had let a lot of time pass them by. Some get lucky and find men within their age bracket but others have to look at a younger age group because what they seek, they can't find in theirs.

Then we have those who are looking for adventure and excitement, that they sure won't get anywhere else but with a younger man.

The reasons why a young lady would date an older man has to do with stability. In her mind, this one has finished 'sowing his wild oats' and he has settled. He will be true to her as long as she plays her cards right. He will provide her financial and emotional needs without demanding too much in return.

For the young men, they feel the older women are more sensible and mature in their dealings. They are more experienced, more focused, there is less unnecessary excitement, they are wiser and more independent.

These are not conclusive facts and the reasons may vary but you and I know that I'm almost completely correct. (Just saying.)

A few of these questions have come up in my research: 1. Why would a woman prefer a younger man to someone within her age group? 2. Does that kind of relationship really work? 3. Can the woman respect the man? 4. What happens if they marry and the woman's age really starts showing, how will it affect their marriage? 5. What will society and family say about a relationship like that?

These are just a few of the most prevalent questions which I came across and I will try as much as I can to tackle them. Like I mentioned before, women go into relationships to basically satisfy their emotional needs and it really doesn't make that much of a difference who satisfies those needs. I am not saying women are easy (never); I'm just saying they know what they want and will overlook as many obstacles as there are, just to get it. If it happens to be a younger man and they are both happy, where's the harm in that?

To answer the question of whether such relationships work, I will say yes, they do, if the couple puts in the work. It's just like every other relationship in life; you don't just sit there after getting into it and expect it to magically grow into something meaningful. The two people involved have to make the decision to fight all the obstacles which will definitely come and make it grow into whatever they expect; it is no piece of cake though.

Now, the question of respect from the woman, knowing that

she is older than the man, truly has to do with the individual and her personality. It doesn't matter who is older or younger in the relationship, if the woman is naturally disrespectful then she can't help it. One way or another, it will pop up and there's nothing much anybody can do about it except she decides on her own to change.

What happens when they marry and her age starts showing? Really? I wasn't aware that some people have a time machine which stops for them at certain times so they can stop aging (being sarcastic again). To the best of my knowledge, everybody ages and it will never change, so let us stop trying to fight what we can never change.

When they were dating, the man knew that he was getting involved with an older woman, he fell madly in love with her still knowing that fact and he went ahead with marrying her so please, let's do ourselves a favour and mind our business.

Your life and happiness shouldn't matter to anyone else but you. The question of how society and family would view your age gap is not important. This is where you can afford to be selfish. Focus on you and your partner and let those who derive pleasure in focusing on you two have a filled day. If you fail at it, then you know you tried and it was not meant to be but not because someone else didn't like it.

Love is a beautiful thing, dear reader! Once you find that one person who makes it all fantastic, you understand how phenomenal it is. You will agree with me then, that something as frivolous as age shouldn't stop you from enjoying this wondrous gift from God. It is your life and anyone who claims to love you would be happy that you are happy. Don't hold back on your love story because he/she is older or younger than you. After all, they say 'age is just a number'.

CHAPTER NINE
SOCIAL MEDIA VERSUS REALITY

The question of whether to expose or not to expose your relationship has been quite recurrent, especially since the world became tinier with social media and everybody has to know everybody's business.

Some people say if a man/woman keeps their relationship hidden, then he/she doesn't really love their partner. Well, people do say a lot of things; however, this chapter is an opportunity to express my opinion on the matter.

Now, before the arrival of social media, people had relationships and they flourished without people knowing about them. Things have changed and we are more digitalised so we can afford to reach more people with the happenings of our lives. It's a great thing but some people have succeeded in turning it into one of those situations where 'too much of something is bad'.

A friend came to me some time ago to show me the messages his girlfriend sent to him. It was actually hilarious but I couldn't laugh in his face due to the seriousness of the situation at the time. She asked him if he was ashamed of her and if she wasn't attractive enough because she couldn't fathom why he wouldn't display her pictures on social media.

I guess I was on a roll that week because another friend who happens to be a very private person, used a woman's picture as his display picture on a social media platform. I got curious because he had never done anything like that before. Heck, I didn't even know he had anyone in his life and we were quite close, or so I thought. Anyway, out of curiosity, I enquired about the lady and he told me she was a lady he had just started seeing but she wouldn't give him a moment of peace because he hadn't used her picture as his display picture. He obviously had to succumb.

Okay listen! This is not supposed to be an issue at all. The most disturbing part of it all is that women are the ones who feel more strongly about this than men. I know that it makes you feel more secure and a lot happier when your man/woman shouts it out to anyone who cares to listen, that you are his/hers (that is actually how it is supposed to be). However, you should learn to take things slowly. Your relationship is still fresh in some cases; you are still getting to really know each other; you haven't even taken time out to process whether this is truly what you want or not and then your biggest problem is not being splashed on social media. Why?

Have you thought about how ridiculous you would feel when the relationship hasn't worked out and you have been published extensively? It hurts a whole lot, especially when you have to explain the breakup over and over again. You really don't want that kind of intrusion into your privacy.

For those who have been in longer relationships, there might be two things involved. Firstly, he/she is a really private person who wants to keep you to himself/herself. The main question to ask is does he/she keep you from his/her inner circle too? If his/her family and friends know you, then you are good but if he/she keeps you away from them too, then it's time to ask yourself some questions.

Secondly, you are not the only person in his/her life and he/she doesn't want all the parties involved to find out about each other. Most of the time in this case, just like I stated in the previous point, you are hidden even from his/her inner circle.

You have to really take time out to evaluate your relationship and see if there are more important things that he/she does to add value to your life, as opposed to acknowledging you publicly. In other words, are there things your partner does for you which you feel are more valuable and important than public acknowledgement of their affection for you, which would make you stay put in the relationship?

If there are, talk to your partner about how you really feel and his/her view would help you make an informed decision on whether to stay or let go.

There is another aspect of this 'social media love' that really bugs me and that is the fact that some people will have a good thing going on in their relationship but because they see what others are putting out there on social media, all of a sudden theirs is not good enough. I simply ask such a person, "Have you completely lost your mind?"

There is a lot of deception in the virtual world nowadays and most people are quick to portray what they are not. Do not pay any heed to those pictures because that is the only affection and attention some of them are getting in those relationships they are so quick to flaunt. After those pictures and videos, they go back into their nightmare. Concentrate on your own journey and enjoy what you have. It is truly not worth losing a good man/woman over.

In my candid opinion, I think displays of affection through pictures and videos should be done after marriage. In fact, your wedding pictures and videos should be the first you display as a couple (if you must). It is exhausting for some of us to see people displaying pictures and tomorrow we hear the two are not together anymore. You can't keep putting the viewers through all that hassle (just kidding). It makes more sense when you are married but don't overdo it because then you become a show-off and start rubbing people up the wrong way. A little privacy is always great.

People! Let's be real! Let's try to live life as simply as it actually is. You are a grown up, so act like it. You can't be hounding another person to display you on social media. You won't really enjoy that forced publicity, I promise you. Let the person decide on his or her own to show you off and you will feel great about it.

CHAPTER TEN
THE BLAME GAME

For as long as I can remember, there has been this back and forth between men and women, especially the younger ones, where the men say women are living up to their standards as daughters of Eve and women say men are the scum of the earth. I wonder how we got here but let's talk about it, shall we?

I'm going to be brutally honest in this chapter and if you can't stomach the truth, then skip to the next chapter, I humbly beg.

I will begin with the men. You have a terrible track record and it scares the living daylight out of me when I hear how far some of you go. I am an honest person and it will be wrong of me to generalise because there exist some really upright and exemplary men. It's sad that the unscrupulous ones just give all men a bad name.

Some men lie so much, that they will surprise even the devil with their expertise. They cheat and deceive women like they weren't born by a woman. You can't help but wonder if they have a conscience at all. It is abysmal.

Now, there are men who got psychologically messed up from childhood because they had no good example from their fathers or older men in their lives. We all know that it is quite easy for children to pick all kinds of habits up as they grow and it happens more quickly, when they spend a lot of time around adults they love.

If a young man had a 'whacky' or irresponsible father or

male figure in his life, he would most likely turn out to be more 'whacky' and irresponsible as a man.

There are those who would have been promising but peer pressure didn't allow it. Men don't really possess a lot of willpower and it is easy to lure them into doing things they didn't plan to do. Their friend is not so nice to women but he gets them anyway and he's so cool; guess what? They want to be cool too and they end up copying the wrong things.

Some men are just pure evil. They have no reason and no excuse but they are just the definition of wickedness. These ones need divine intervention or else they will drive you to insanity.

At first, I was empathetic and tried to make excuses for the ones who walked into my life and the lives of those close to me but one day, I woke up to the fact that there is no excuse for being mean.

She is a woman and you are lucky to have her in your life. She just wants to be loved and treated with respect. If we really examine it and put the two of you on a scale, you would see that you seriously hit jackpot with her and you don't deserve a woman like that. She is way above your league but she has put aside many things, sacrificed much more just to be with you; yet you don't see it.

Most men specialise in seeing only the wrong things their women do and are first to dish out compliments to other people, who have done nothing to deserve all the praise. There are those who will not even give their women gifts to show appreciation or even provide for her no matter how small, to show he at least cares. Then some guy gives her a little of what you have been busy denying her and you won't stop ranting and calling her and the entire womenfolk names.

Stop looking for who to blame for your problems. The

extreme display of cowardice is sad. It's not working or it's not what I thought it was going to be, so the best thing is to call it quits immediately and jump to the next woman. Mr. Froggy, you will be jumping about for a very long time if you don't get your act together.

Put in the work and be patient. Give your relationship time to grow and mature. You are a man, so please act like it and stop with the childish excuses and if you do not want to grow up, stick to your video games and stop inviting women into your confused world.

Now ladies! Ladies! Ladies! I understand that you have been at the receiving end of a lot of meanness and disrespect for a long time. It is enough to damage anyone with blood running through their veins. It hurts so bad to give your heart to a man and then it is returned to you in pieces; then you manage to mend it and it comes back in pieces again.

However, the reason why it doesn't work most of the time is that you didn't give yourself enough time to heal properly from one heartbreak and bad relationship, before jumping into another one. You carry the hurt, pain and baggage to another person without taking time to figure out what your part in the bad relationship was. Truth is; you had a part to play in how messed up things got but we are always quick to shift the blame. You ignored the signs and closed your ears to the truth.

The fact that you were committed and caring to Tom and he messed up, doesn't mean you should become cold and calculating to Andrew. It will only bring out the worst in Andrew and he will show you another side of him you never knew existed. You break up and Andrew has issues with all women because of you, without knowing you were just acting on past hurt. You go out there and spit more venom on another person because all men are scum. You see what is happening? It becomes a never-ending circle of bitterness, retaliation and pain.

Guys, let's stop the blame game. Every one of us has a part to play in how messed up things have become but it is not irreparable. You can fix that relationship you think is hopeless, simply by giving it one more chance and readjusting your methods. And if you feel it's not worth the fight, then get out before things get too deep and complicated; then think about what you need to change before you jump into another relationship.

CHAPTER ELEVEN
COMMUNICATION

Imagine a world where we move about without telling each other: how and what we feel, what we need and when we need it, what we like and dislike. It sucks right? That is what we do in relationships and it is a disease that needs to be eradicated.

Maryanne and Desmond had been dating for two years and I would rate their relationship as average because they were two very busy people who hardly spent time together. However, they loved each other deeply but the time apart didn't allow them to get to know each other as well as they should have. When issues arose, each one would make outrageous assumptions and draw conclusions instead of talking about it. They kept getting it wrong and their relationship took a downward spiral.

Too many unfortunate incidents took place and they broke up briefly; they didn't take the separation too well, so they found their way back to each other. This time, they decided to do things differently and they talked about everything they had not disclosed in the past. They made sure to communicate every day, even with their busy schedules. They decided never to hide their feelings and thoughts from each other. This opened a new dimension to their relationship as they discovered new things about themselves each day.

Desmond and Maryanne's story is common in many relationships and it has crashed many good unions.

Communication is very important in every relationship on earth and can't be overemphasised. We communicate with our family members, we communicate with our friends and we communicate with our colleagues at work; on official and non-official duties. So, why can't we communicate properly with our partners whom we claim to love?

To begin with, this person cannot possibly know what you are going through or what you feel if you do not open up to them. Sometimes, there is the fear of how your communication would be received and so the best option is to hold it in. Hell no! If you cannot freely talk to your man/woman about your concerns, feelings and thoughts, then you don't have any business being with that person in the first place.

Good communication builds trust between two people because it lets each person know that you have completely let them into your life and it gives them an air of worthiness. Whatever guard they had up is automatically let down, because there's a feeling of complete trust. There is transparency in the relationship and no room for unnecessary lies and deceit.

Someone once asked me if there are any restrictions on what to communicate about or should we just put everything on the table? In other words, what and what not to communicate about. Well, there are no set rules anywhere but I think it depends on how much you as an individual are ready to let out. Talk about your feelings for your partner (trust me, they never get tired of hearing it), talk about the things which upset you, talk about your goals and aspirations, talk about the future. This gives your partner, a chance to evaluate you better; particularly if it's a man who intends to marry you. It will enable him to picture the future better (don't you think?).

You need to be sure about where the relationship is truly heading before you go blurting out too much though. Don't go too deep if the relationship is not too serious yet or if you feel your partner can't handle certain truths. Keep your unsavoury past to yourself. I said communicate properly and not be silly. Use your head and gauge the situation properly; if it's something which could potentially harm a good relationship then keep quiet and let bygones be bygones.

When to communicate: I know I mentioned earlier that communication should be free flowing but it doesn't mean you should call your partner at work to tell him a sob story of your first dog that died years ago and how you just got emotional about it. No! Choose the time wisely for certain topics. If the two of you are on a date, talk about your feelings; if you are at work, make sure it is a quick hello and get back to work; after work, talk about your day in general.

Ladies! It is important to note that men are big babies and when communicating certain dislikes or things which got you really upset, you need to be careful with your presentation or else they will misunderstand you and call you a nag. (They just love that word 'nag'.)

In the heat of the moment you may be so upset you want to scream but don't. Take a moment to calm down. Take deep breaths and count to ten; trust me, it's an effective relaxing technique. You will notice how much your approach will change towards the situation and how much drama you will have avoided.

Guys! Note that women are very emotional and our hormones are always running haywire so please handle with care. If you do not know what to say and when to say it; bite your tongue. The last thing you want is the wrong words coming out of your mouth, because you will be astonished at the reaction you will get.

Communication has been made so easy these days with calls, texts, WhatsApp, DMs, FaceTime and it looks like there will be much more in the near future, so seriously, what's your excuse, again?

CHAPTER TWELVE
WHAT DO WE REALLY WANT?

Men and women have always wanted to know what each one wants and it is all very intriguing. I find it hard to understand both sexes sometimes as well, because I look at some couples and see that they have a wonderful thing going on but they don't see it themselves; hence, things keep going wrong. I see some other couples who have no business being together but they are holding on tight for the most absurd reasons. I completely agree that all of the complications are enough to ask each other what we really want.

Before I attempt to answer this very pertinent question, I need to first point out that you, as a: person, human being, living organism need to figure out what you want, as opposed to what you need.

For example: The norm is for a man to get a good, well-cultured, well-bred, Christian girl who will respect him in every way and love him right; that is exactly what he needs to be a happy and fulfilled man. Meanwhile, the same man wants a good, Christian yet fun-loving and adventurous girl to make him a happy and fulfilled man. What do you think will happen when he lands with category A? Exactly! It will be a big flop. It is important to note this fact because it worked for many people I know and it has worked for me too. Always choose what you want, for there lies your happiness.

Having said all of that, let me shed some light on what men and women truly want, in my opinion.

Men want to be respected. A woman has to be careful how she talks to her man and how she behaves towards her man in private and in public. It is an established fact, that men are the head and that position will never switch, no matter how big, tall or successful the woman is. Always remind yourselves ladies; he is the head. I know sometimes they don't quite exhibit their leadership qualities properly but do not make the mistake of undermining the fact that they lead and we follow.

Men do not want women who joke with their very fragile egos. A man's ego is very important to him. It's like a second skin and they are sensitive about it; so, the moment you take a wrong step and wound their ego, you are gone. That ego of theirs is what makes them stand proud as men and you want to burst that bubble too? Common!

To stroke a man's ego isn't difficult; compliment him as much as you can but don't lie just to please him; no matter how independent you are as a woman, allow him take care of you; listen to him and don't shrug off what he says for any reason; show up when he needs you and support him always in all he does.

Men want alone time. Ladies! Sometimes, we do too much. Let the man breathe, please! He needs time to think, time to work, time to relax, time to discover places on his own, time to bond with his friends, time to miss you. Give the man some alone time; he truly needs it and you need it as well. Stop following men wherever they go and at all times, because you are choking him and he will soon get irritated.

Men want to be loved. Forget the hard exterior that men portray all the time; a man will latch on to a woman he can be vulnerable with and whom he feels loves him the way he craves to be loved. Men were taught from childhood that they are tough but the woman in his life represents that soft cushion he can relax on and he truly doesn't joke with that. Men are loved differently, so learn what your man's emotional needs are and love him accordingly.

Men want trust. I know it seems unfair that some men do a fine job of breaking a woman's trust over and over again and you are supposed to forgive them seventy times seven, like the Bible says but trust is extremely important to men. So much so that once you break it, they will find it very hard to forgive you. Be careful with your actions because men are smart and they will eventually get to know. Once a man is certain he can trust you, he will let his guard down and let you in completely.

Men want mystery. Don't be too quick to give everything away; leave room for a man to wonder about you. Mystery is what makes some men cheat. The other woman leaves him begging for more simply because she gives him everything in tiny doses. Don't be boring or systematic. Continually whet his appetite for you and thank me later.

Women's wants are a bit similar to men's but different at the same time. A woman is more emotional, so once you win her heart, you are halfway through.

Women want communication. You need to constantly check on them, talk to them and hear them out. When you cut the flow of communication with a woman, her imagination starts running very wild and there are dire consequences.

Women want attention. Always make time for your woman when she needs you. A woman who gets attention glows from within, because she knows that she can always count on you no matter how tight your schedule is, to make time for her. By the way, no man is busy twenty-four hours a day, so stop with the lies.

A woman wants care and kindness. How can you say you love someone and not care for and about the person? It's not possible so please, go out of your way to show how much you care about her and perform random acts of kindness. You will melt her heart completely.

A woman wants you to respect her mind, her career, her interests and her body. Do not belittle her in anyway. Respecting her shows how much value your place in your woman's life. Respecting her also gives room for others in your life to respect her as well and that is a major score.

A woman wants consistency. You bought flowers in the beginning, well, keep buying flowers. You took her out on dates before, you better continue. You were Mr. Romantic when the relationship started, keep being that. You were faithful at first, please don't stop. A woman doesn't want you to stop being the man she met in the beginning so stick to that script, will you? Things start getting ugly when you completely change into a person she no longer recognises. I know life happens and circumstances may force a person to change in some ways but let her still see a hint of the man she fell in love with.

There you have it! There are so many wants from both sexes but those not mentioned in this chapter would best be discussed between you and your partner. However, if you follow these few, I bet you will enjoy the peace and joy that you will start noticing in your relationship.

CHAPTER THIRTEEN
LOVE AND DISTANCE

For many people, making their relationship work is actually 'work', which takes a lot of time and effort and it is made a bit easier because you get to see the person often and watch the fruits of your labour blossom before your very eyes. Now, when your partner is in a different town, city or country, it becomes more of a challenge.

Most times, some of these relationships don't start off as long-distance because the people involved met, liked each other and dated for a while before the separation happened. In this case, the foundation of the relationship is a little bit solid and some memories have been created together, which reinforces the invisible pull between the two when they are separated.

It is this pull which makes them want to do everything they possibly can to make the relationship work, as opposed to their counterparts who either met online or through matchmaking. Let me explain the matchmaking part for some of you who look a bit confused. Well, an example would be James who lives in Nigeria and is single but is seriously searching for a good girl to start a serious relationship with. He has an aunt who has been living in Ghana and knows this very good girl named Alice, who would be perfect for her nice nephew (according to her). She tells James about Alice and the two get connected and 'boom', they actually like each other. Now, you get it?

For the latter set of people, it is a bigger challenge because they met from afar; they are trying to get to know each other from afar and they have not even seen each other in most cases and have no prior history. The progress of this type of relationship depends a lot on how much work each partner is willing to put in. Difficult but not impossible and I will tell you why…

Whether you have been together before separation or you met online, one of the key things is to be open and honest to each other about what you expect from the relationship. Let the other person have a clear picture of what they are getting into so they know how to buckle up. Long-distance relationships are no joke and definitely not for the faint-hearted; it is different from regular relationships where you can watch the evolution of the relationship on a daily basis. You can't tie another person down when you know you are just not ready for anything serious and you know they are too far from you to figure it out on their own. You will agree with me that it would be unfair.

These days, we have been blessed with how much technology has brought everyone closer and made people more accessible. Use every means of communication which suits the two of you as much as possible. Communication cannot be overemphasised because it is basically all you have as a sustenance tool. However, you don't have to always talk. (I know! Sounds contradictory.) This means it is good to leave room for some mystery in the relationship.

Whatever you do and however crazy your schedule is, I beg you to make time, as often as possible, to visit each other. It is very important. The saying that out of sight is out of mind is true, when he or she just doesn't get to see you. The texts are sweet, the calls will make their day, the pictures are a great reminder of you but your actual presence is unforgettable.

To those who met online, I know you are trying to make a great impression with the pictures you put up on your profile but please relax with the over-editing and filters. Make sure that when you two meet for the first time, you actually look like 'you', otherwise you can definitely forget about that relationship you have succeeded in building for all those months. Be as transparent and as natural as you can be.

Be creative and romantic when you have the opportunity to be together. Those memories you create at that time are the memories your partner will take with them when they leave. Don't make the mistake of using that time to catch up on work or be too serious. Go all out of your comfort zones and be crazy.

Intimacy should be kept alive in a long distance relationship. He/she is not your business partner or work colleague. Flirt with each other and make sure to keep the spark between you two alive.

If you happen to have kids together, I understand that you may have a lot of family issues to discuss but also fit some intimate details about the two of you somewhere in there.

Yes, your day was long and stressful and she sympathises with you wholeheartedly but that is not the only reason she waited for your call for all those hours.

It will be hard and frustrating sometimes, you will want to give up many times, you will wonder what in God's name you were thinking but hold on tight. It is neither easy in regular nor long-distance relationships but it always boils down to how determined you are to making a good relationship last.

CHAPTER FOURTEEN
INFIDELITY AND EXCLUSIVITY

This chapter is one I have been a little bit worried about writing because the pain caused, which is still being caused on a daily basis, by the topic of infidelity, aches me down to my soul.

I feel like we should stop giving reasons for why people cheat because there is no justifiable reason for anyone to debase themselves by living a pretentious, morally depraving and disgusting life, because they feel it is a better option than just putting in a little extra effort into making it work with the person who is giving you their all.

Fine! Let us discuss why people cheat, just to satisfy their justification, shall we?

Women say they cheated because they were not given enough attention and care. They felt so alone in the relationship. They didn't feel the love that existed between them and their partner anymore. They felt underappreciated. They craved intimacy.

Their male counterparts on the other hand cheat because they are: immature, selfish, sexually enthusiastic, have deep issues from childhood, insecure, angry or depressed, cowards, tired of being nagged constantly and looking for an escape.

There are many books and websites dedicated to explaining this topic in detail and trying really hard to break it down into many parts to make it less annoying and I say kudos to them for a job well done. However, I feel we have done enough talking about cheaters and why they cheat.

What causes me to ache the most is how much technology has come to contribute to making a bad situation worse. You see full grown men tip toeing around just to answer calls or freaking out when their partner so much as touches their phones. They spend money which could be used in more profitable ventures, to spoil some girl who doesn't give a hoot about them for real.

You have a house but your partner may just pop in at any time, so let's go to some cheap hotel somewhere and expose ourselves to more filth and depravity. Well, that's for people with a little shame because the proud and serial cheaters would take the women to their homes, partner be damned.

Cheater ladies, don't think I forgot you! You have been so lonely so you sneak out to go and meet the person you feel will give you twenty-four hours loving. You feel underappreciated and you think the big guy is just out to sing your praises all day, because he is that jobless. He has plans too and once he gets what he wants, you will be lonelier and be more underappreciated.

Look, if you feel you are tired of him/her and can't stomach how they make you feel: GET OUT. It's that simple. What are you doing hanging on to someone who makes you feel like less of a person? Someone who openly hurts you and is not even remorseful about it? Get out and break free from all of that, because it is not worth it.

Some people choose to endure and tolerate and see where it ends. I get that because I have been on that road. There are some men who cheat and you know they did it because of some lame reason (which is no excuse at all); but their daily efforts in trying to show you how much they are willing to make it up to you, is enough reason to give it one last shot.

There are women who cheat and get burned and they realise their mistakes as well. Weigh the situation up properly and pray for discernment from God to be able to tell which signs are genuine and which are fake. You can never do it on your own, so rely solely on prayers.

Let me tell you one highly ignored truth; God hates ugly. I am yet to see anyone who cheated on their undeserving partners go scot-free. There is always a price to pay and it is never pretty. Look around and ask questions and you will see I'm right. It never ends well. I won't sit here and tell you to stop cheating or why you should stop, because you are a grown up but I will remind you that if you do not stop, there are repercussions and you will live to regret it.

At this point in your life, you have attained a certain level of maturity and you know yourself, my brother/sister. If you are incapable of being exclusive in a relationship (being with only one partner, just so we are clear), do yourself a favour and either stay away from good girls/guys whose hearts you will surely break *or* make it clear to the ladies/gents that you cannot be exclusive, so that they make an informed decision to stay or go.

If you feel you are brave and noble enough to stick to one person, then you have to put up a fight because temptation will surely come and your assignment would then be learning how to flee from it. I watched a program a while ago and this young man said something which really touched me. They were a young couple and he was a part-time student. In his school, he kept seeing all these women and the temptation was high, of course. Instead of indulging, what he did was to tell his wife about it. She was a wise, young lady because she didn't attack him and say something ignorant such as, 'Why were you looking in the first place? Couldn't you just look away?' Instead, she thanked him for being honest and they prayed about it. Now, this man knows that he has an open door with his wife and can come to her for anything. Such honesty is powerful. You will say that is a case involving marriage and not all women will be like the lady. Yeah, yeah, yeah but try it first and see. You cannot say something is impossible when you have not tried it.

Let's stop with the excuses for our bad behavior because frankly, it's getting old. You have so much to give to your partner, to your dreams and aspirations, to your family and society. There is no value in chasing women of all shapes and sizes, just to make yourself feel better and there is no pride in jumping around from one man to the other, to feel emotionally fulfilled. If you check and he/she is not putting in any effort to make it work with you, leave. You will see how quickly you meet that special person who will make your dreams come true.

CHAPTER FIFTEEN
BABY BOY/GIRL VERSUS REAL MAN/WOMAN

So many of us go about life meeting the wrong set of people and when things go wrong as expected, they start pointing fingers at every member of that particular sex as if they were all in it. This chapter is going to help differentiate certain classes of people to help you, my dear readers, make the right choices (or what appear to be the right choices).

Baby boys are those men who get stuck in the young and silly stage. When you first meet them, you will get enchanted by their mischievous, adventurous spirit; but look past that, I beg you.

They are actually quite interesting and everything just seems to happen around them all the time. Truth is, that is all they have to offer you. Don't be fooled by the 'living larger than life' façade because they have no clue what life is truly about. Being with such a person is risky because no matter how grown up they may seem, they will never understand it until they decide to truly mature on their own. You should expect a lot of rebellion from them, because they love their life the way it is and don't want you meddling.

Baby boys don't take responsibility for anything: they don't care if you are hurt or feeling bad, they don't care if you have needs, they get you pregnant but they don't care about you or the baby. Oh, I was a bit wrong about one fact and that is that they care about something: themselves! They are the most selfish set of people on earth. If it works for them, then they are in but if they are not getting anything out of it, they don't want it at all.

Baby boys are cowards in the real sense of the word. They will run away from what might not even be a real challenge. They don't know how to stay and fight because they are weak.

Baby boys have the most annoying sense of entitlement. They feel they deserve everything: nice and beautiful. It's their right and you have to bow to all their whims and caprices and if you don't, well, there are many fish in the sea. They won't lift a finger for you but want you to turn the world upside down for them.

Baby boys are the kings of reasons and excuses. They are also the smoothest liars. It's like second nature to them. They can spin the most convincing tale and you will believe it. They are that good, trust me. You need to be extremely vigilant and careful when you are dating a baby boy, so that you don't fall into his deceitful web.

There are fewer real men these days but they exist. In case you were still wondering and for those who don't know how to spot one, here are some pointers to guide you.

Real men are natural leaders: they take charge, they get the job done without questions, they know what to do and when to do it, they understand the value of time and refuse to waste it, they are very organised and conscientious.

Real men are respectful. They respect people in general and they definitely respect women if for no other reason, just for being the wonderful creatures that they truly are. They portray respect in the way they talk to women, the way they protect women and the way they defend women.

Real men are honest. Sometimes I would say; brutally honest. That is just because they prefer to hurt you with the truth than tell a lie.

Real men are hardworking and ambitious. It might not be rosy at the moment or they may not have reached the heights they want to get to but they don't stop trying. They keep working and achieving goals and fulfilling their dreams.

Real men support their women. He will show up for you whenever you need him. He supports his woman's career, his woman's dreams and he helps her to achieve them. He supports the choices she makes because he trusts her judgement.

Real men are emotionally intelligent. He knows how to react to his woman's feelings. He is able to discern her ever-changing moods and knows how to behave, to avoid 'setting his woman off'. He knows what to say and when to say it.

Real men know how to prioritise. They know who owns each place in their lives and they make sure not to get wires crossed, so that their friends don't take more priority than their woman, their job doesn't take more priority than their family. They give everyone their dues.

Real men apologise when they are wrong. They don't walk around with the invisible 'I'm a man' sign hanging from their necks. They take responsibility for what they have done wrong, apologise and try to make things right.

Real men are not afraid or ashamed to be romantic. They show how much they love you wherever the occasion presents itself. They want to show you off and let the world know how special you are as their woman. They just thrive in putting smiles on the face of the woman they love.

Baby girls and their male counterparts are similar in many ways. They are unreasonable, unrealistic, immature and irresponsible. They are too superficial and exist in their own world where everything is shiny and easy. They, however, get into situations which force them to grow up faster than the baby boys, most of the time. They are lazy and unnaturally stubborn. They are selfish and dishonest.

Real women learn quite early that they can be their own boss and they strive to achieve their goals and build their dreams on their own. They can survive quite well in any situation and they will handle anything with true dignity and grace.

Real women are nurturing and giving. They don't rest until everyone around them is doing okay and is happy.

Real women are forgiving. Don't get it wrong, they are hurting really badly but they will forgive you quickly, because they believe in letting things go.

Real women are patient and kind. They are not in a hurry because they believe that at the right time, things always fall into place.

Real women are faithful. They respect their body and treasure it so much, that they will readily keep it for the one person they truly love.

Real women are intelligent and smart. It is difficult to trick a real woman because she sees you coming from afar. She is very wise as well and would always give you good counsel.

A real woman is very loving. There is no length and breadth that she won't cover, to make sure her man, her kids, her family, her friends and colleagues are happy.

As always, these are pointers and they are subjective. They are just to help give you a better idea about the different kinds of men/women that exist in our world, especially in the present day. It's sad that most people keep meeting the baby boys and girls but there are some really awesome men and women out there.

That you haven't met him/her yet, doesn't mean they don't exist or are not on the lookout for a great person like you as well.

Most of us are so impatient but I understand your loneliness and frustration. I am a great believer in there being a woman for every man and vice versa. Don't give up.

While you are waiting, keep working on yourself and living your best life. Always keep in mind that your happiness begins with you. Go out and explore your options. You don't want him/her to walk into your life and meet a sad and depressed person but a vivacious and life-loving person.

CHAPTER SIXTEEN
BREAK-UPS AND MOVING ON

I have often wondered why there is no scientific or medical name given to the pain associated with break-ups; that pain is indescribable. Those who were in love and broke up can relate. It hits you as if a building collapsed right on top of you and you just can't breathe.

How does it get to the point where two people, who in some cases are clearly crazy about each other, decide to go their separate ways? Let's try to break it down.

Relationships are sometimes scary. That is simply because there's no way of actually knowing what to really expect as time goes on. Everyone is just going about thinking they have it all figured out but in reality, who can tell who is and who is not getting it right? You think it would be enough to just fall in love with that beautiful lady or handsome man and do stuff together and everything will be forever rosy but it is not.

Life happens, pressure from different angles attack you, monotony descends on you and everyone is bored all of a sudden, you start despising things you thought you liked at first, misunderstandings are the order of the day and no one is actually talking about the real problems or one person is talking and the other just won't listen. It's a huge mess.

Even the strongest people crack when things get to such a chaotic point and I want you, my dear reader, to know it's normal and you are not insane for feeling as low as you do when it gets ugly. It happens in every relationship.

The one thing you need to get out of your head before getting into any relationship is that there exists a 'perfect relationship'. It might look perfect in the beginning but it doesn't last too long before reality sets in, so you need to brace yourself. That thought pattern is not supposed to scare you or make you live with negative vibes, it is supposed to empower you so that you can stand and fight whatever ugly challenges come in the future.

Most of us refuse vehemently to leave our fantasy world and see the truth and then one day, it gets to the point where we are saying goodbye to the person who was the reason for our happiness. Let's stop all of that and be realistic.

There are too many reasons why people break up and each relationship has its story and I am not here to give you twenty reasons why people break up. Ask Google. However, I will shed some light on a few things you should do, if you believe in your heart that you love the person and you are ready to truly commit to the relationship and, of course, don't want a break-up.

Firstly, stop being selfish. It is not about you all the time. You have another person in your life and his/her feelings should be considered and made a priority. Stop assuming things and drawing unnecessary conclusions. Try to understand the other person's point of view. When you allow yourself to stop making everything about you, it allows you to see situations differently and you become more rational.

Please ask questions and seek clarifications as opposed to bottling them up inside and causing the foundation of your relationship to crack more and more. I mean, how difficult is it? This person is the woman/man you love; how hard can it be to ask them to explain themselves better. You deserve to know and they will feel better when they get you to understand their reason for doing certain things they do, which put you off. Communicate people, communicate!

When you are angry, please shut up 'til further notice. Avoid letting stuff drop from your lips in the heat of the moment because you will say something horrible and most likely unforgettable. Bite your tongue and leave the scene immediately.

Now, I didn't say go to a place which will make you vulnerable to temptation like a bar or an admirer's house; instead, go to that one friend who represents a sounding board in your life. The one who is not afraid to look you in the eye and tell the truth. Just take the time to cool off and you will see how easily your perception of the whole situation changes.

Break-ups are nasty. They have destroyed some people's lives because they were in denial and wanted to do everything to keep living like the break-up didn't happen, until the day they are forced to face the ugly truth. Some others go on a vengeful mission and try to do stuff to get their ex back for putting them through the pain. Some have been so tainted by a bad break-up that they have refused to open themselves up to what would have been beautiful relationships.

Moving on is never easy. You had a deep connection with this person. You shared so many beautiful moments together and you are just supposed to switch the 'off' button automatically? It is not possible. It takes a long and painful time.

For those who have broken up, please stay away from people who will readily tell you to 'get over it already'. They haven't even healed properly from their own experiences, trust me. Take your time to heal. Avoid places which remind you of your ex as much as possible and if you had mutual friends, avoid them too. At least for a while.

If the break-up was not due to something you did, then please do not make the mistake of letting your ex ever see you looking miserable. Make sure that you become a better, hotter and happier version of you before seeing him/her again. You want to leave your ex looking at you and wondering what in the world they were thinking by leaving you. That is the greatest and best healing tonic.

You can do it. Get out of that dark room and acquire a new skill or follow a new passion. Go meet your guys for drinks at your favourite spot. Get a new haircut or change that hairstyle. You have great legs, flaunt them tastefully. Anyone who left a special person like you, doesn't deserve more tears than necessary. I know it is hard but you can do it.

And for you who left a good man/woman because of some unreasonable reasons; well, that was your mistake and you won't find anything better. They will always realise it in the end but it is often too late then. You don't want to go through all of that now, do you?

I have an exercise which has always helped me make tough decisions a bit easier and I want you to do it. You feel like things have reached a dead end and you can't take it anymore. The best thing is for each person to go their own way; just hold on for a minute. Get comfortable and do this when you are alone. Close your eyes and take seven deep breaths just to help you relax. I want you to go down memory lane and see how far you and your partner have come; all the challenges you overcame together and all the memories made. Start erasing your partner in each memory and try to imagine what would have happened in those situations if they were not in the picture. Now, imagine them gone for good.

If the picture without them looks scary then fight for your relationship because it's worth fighting for but if you rather prefer them out of the picture, then break it off and stop wasting each other's time.

CHAPTER SEVENTEEN
SECOND TIME AROUND

When a couple breaks up, there is always this question of whether they would ever get back together, which lingers for a while. I don't know if it is because the onlookers are not convinced about the break-up or they just don't understand how all of a sudden, two people they knew as a great couple would part ways in a flash.

Whatever the case, the break-up happened but like I always say, you can't escape true love and they often find their way back to each other. Most likely, it was just a badly handled misunderstanding which made them drift apart and not that they didn't love each other. This case is less dramatic and easier to understand.

The people I want to focus on in this chapter, are those who hurt someone deeply, then there was a break-up, then there was realisation that a huge mistake had been made, then forgiveness and reconciliation was sought and then they came back together.

People don't realise how much of a psychological and emotional torture hurt can be. It is like a big wound which keeps getting bigger if not handled properly and they think by saying the famous 'I'm sorry', it magically fixes everything; well, it doesn't. Which explains why some people find it really hard to let go because just looking at the person who hurt them every day is too much of a reminder and they prefer to permanently shut that door. They have forgiven you quite all right but they just can't handle being around you for too long, for fear of what it might do to them or make them do to you.

However, there are those who are stronger and who love deeper and they choose to brave it a second time or in some cases a third time with the person who hurt them and I respect that. It is not an easy decision to make but it is made easier by how the second time around is handled.

I will begin with the one who offended. I don't know what it is that you did that was horrible enough to cause a rift between your partner and yourself but it is commendable that you realised your mistakes and went to make amends and get him/her back.

Now, you have them back but you are like someone walking on egg shells because the next mistake might be the end of it. Take a mental inventory of all the things you did wrong the first time. Try to remember the things your partner complained about incessantly and you ignored at the time. Become a version of yourself which would remind your partner of the person they fell in love with in the beginning.

This is a trying time, I know; you feel horrible sometimes because it looks like the more you try, the less impact it has on how your partner feels but it is important to be very patient. Time will heal all of it if you do things right and before long, you will have a stronger bond than you had the first time. It doesn't happen overnight so, take things slowly.

Sometimes, your partner would get into a fit of rage because they are a bit bitter; allow them to vent as much as possible. Let them get it out of their system and they will feel better. No matter how hurtful some of their words may be, do not make the mistake of turning it into an argument at that moment. It is a difficult situation but you will be all right.

Now, to the offended, I know you are hurting and it is true that you forgave them but it just doesn't feel like that is enough -

but it is. By forgiving and loving your partner enough to go back, you have taken a huge step. Don't let yourself be consumed by bitterness, because it destroys the soul. Let your mind be at ease because in actual fact, you WON and that is the reason they came looking for you with their tail between their legs. Let it go and make the second time around count for something.

The bad memories don't fade away overnight. They keep haunting you but don't let it be a reason why each time you see your partner, you bring up what they did to you. Women do that a lot and it is understandably painful. This would only make your partner feel really bad and cause you two to drift farther apart. It is important to tune your mind to the efforts they are making presently, as this will speed up the healing process. If you must bring up hurtful stuff from the past, do it with wisdom and in a subtle way so that your partner truly understands how that situation made you feel. It becomes more of a conversation than a confrontation.

You are not completely innocent when it comes to how your relationship took a bad turn the first time. Try to figure out how and where you made mistakes and come up with better tactics on how to correct them.

Look, you both love each other and that was the connection which pulled you back into each other's lives; don't mess this new opportunity up. Communicate more than ever about any and everything and rebuild trust. It is not going to be easy but trust me, you can do it and you will be happy that you did.

CHAPTER EIGHTEEN
KEEPING THE RIGHT COMPANY

Friends! Friends! Friends! We can't escape them because we need them in our lives, whether we like it or not. There are some people who claim they are fine on their own and don't need friends, they even come up with a long list of reasons why their claim is justified but I say that is 'crap'. At one point or the other in your life, you have had a friend, have a friend and will have a friend.

Like everything in life, there is the good and the bad; hence, there are good friends and bad ones. It is a risky business because there is no way of instantly telling if a person would be a good or bad friend but time always reveals all of that when a person's true nature surfaces. There are a few pointers to help you decide what category your friend belongs to but as always; these are my observations.

A true friend will be unapologetically honest with you. They will hit you hard with the truth and it might leave your head spinning. This type of honesty is born from the deep love they have for you. They don't care if you hate them afterwards but they prefer you to know the truth. A bad friend will sugarcoat it in the guise of not wanting to hurt you because they still want to keep you in their lives for their selfish reasons.

A true friend is fiercely loyal. They have your back at any point in time and will defend you in your presence and absence. It is quite painful that loyalty is on the decrease these days and betrayal is the order of the day.

A true friend supports you in everything you do. They may not like the decisions you make and try to talk you out of it sometimes but they will always show up for you. Bad friends only show up when they will gain something from it and when it is convenient for them.

In relationships, the kind of friends you keep is a huge factor. We have the supportive friends who will cheer your relationship on and act as mediators, when they notice there is a misunderstanding between you and your partner. They just love seeing you two together and feel they should do whatever necessary to help keep your relationship going strong. Provided they give good and reasonable advice; these are the kind of friends you should keep.

There are friends whom I call the 'influencers'; these ones are like silent poison. They come in and try to dictate how things should be run in your own affairs simply because you let them. Most of them do not have solid or meaningful relationships of their own, so I always wonder where they gathered their vast knowledge from. Sadly, they have a smooth way of getting into a person's head and controlling them. Beware of this kind.

There are the 'it's none of my business' kind of friends. I understand that a person's relationship is their private business and you should stay away unless you have been invited in but there are some cases where you *should* 'butt' in to save a bad situation. This set of people will prefer to see you drown in sorrow, than lift a finger to save you from unnecessary pain. This one is for the men in particular.

Let me give you an example to help you understand the point I made above. Arnold had been cheating on Francisca for a while and his friends all knew about it. I found out too and was shocked that no one was saying anything. Don't get me wrong, I'm not a tattletale and I wouldn't just run to an already broken woman, to tell her that her man was seeing someone else seriously on the side. I expected his friends to call him to order but when I asked them, they said it was none of their business.

It was, however, their business when Francisca would spend hours in the kitchen cooking for them to come to eat. It was their business when she would drive from point A to point B to come and drive them home because they had had too much to drink. It was their business when they went out with Arnold and his side-piece to some bar but it was none of their business when it was the right thing to call their friend, sit him down and talk some sense into him.

They call it a code but I call it arrant nonsense. The fact that you are celebrating your friend doing something wrong, encourages that friend to keep digging his grave. If you stand up to him as his 'guys', it will get him thinking in the right direction, because men value their friends' opinions.

His ego may not allow him to accept what you tell him at that moment but he will think about it. This has destroyed many relationships; the fact that nobody agreed to step up and speak up to ensure that they don't ruin their friendship. You could actually shoot two birds with one stone by keeping your friendship and saving a relationship. Isn't that a better offer?

When women go telling their friends that they caught their man doing something wrong, society frowns at it and everybody starts blaming them. I know they gossip and some women really cross the line sometimes but I understand why they do it. Women have mastered the art of putting themselves in their fellow woman's place, so her first instinct is to let her friend know, so she can take the necessary steps to curtail an already ugly situation.

It is high time that we become aware that we need to tastefully help each other in this race. All of us are doing the best we can but if we get the right kind of support sometimes, it helps a great deal.

Another very vital point is that we should choose the kind of friends we hang out with when we realise that the relationship has become pretty serious.

You cannot be with friends who are in no relationship whatsoever and you expect them to understand how much your life has changed. Nobody says you should dump your friends but it is time to practice what I call 'separation of powers'. Put everyone in their rightful place. Every once in a long while you can hang out with this group of friends but there's always the likelihood that the places they would like to go to, are places which will put you in trouble. Remember; they are still hunting.

It is advisable to look through your list of friends and choose people who have good relationships. These ones would speak your kind of language and you will understand each other.

Friends are amazing when you have them in your life but you need to be more mature in choosing who stays in your life when you are in a relationship, because their input could either make or mar what you have going on.

CHAPTER NINETEEN
ALONE TIME

What do you do when you are on your own? Does it make you feel great or you hate it? Well, I love my 'me time' and I always use the time to relax and reflect. I have made the best decisions of my life when I was on my own and I am guessing that most people love taking time to be on their own as well.

I know you want to spend time with your family, with your friends, your colleagues and especially your man/woman because it is a lot of fun and it is heartwarming but there are huge benefits to staying on your own too.

Firstly, it gives you time to reconnect with yourself. In the hurried world we live in nowadays, it is easy to get caught up and you forget that you are an actual living being. You forget what dreams and aspirations you had in the past. You forget how it feels to sit and watch a good movie on your own. You forget how invigorating a good book can be. You could even sleep and relax and feel brand new when you wake up. You see? It doesn't sound so bad now, does it?

Secondly, being alone is the right time to tune in with God. You don't have to be a pastor or prophet to take time out to have deep communication with God. I don't think you are an atheist, so you agree that life without God is meaningless. Catch up on the daily devotion you have not had all week because of work. Pray fervently for yourself and loved ones. You will see the impact this has on your spiritual, emotional and mental lives respectively.

Thirdly, being alone gives you an opportunity to see things more clearly. You may have said something in anger but didn't realise at that point that what you said could have harmed the other person but when you take time alone to think, it will hit you. You generally would come up with the best ideas and best plans during this time because no one is breathing down your neck or nagging you about one thing or the other.

You know who loves their alone time more than everyone else? MEN.

Contrary to what we the women think; men are quite simple. The key is to know what exactly they are in the mood for at a particular moment and you give it to them. If you didn't get all of that, let me explain using this scenario: A young man has spent five exhausting days giving his all to his work and it has been quite rewarding and he can't complain but his plan is to spend Saturday morning in bed, just to catch up on some much-needed sleep. Then he decides to hang out with his friend William in the evening as another means of relaxation. Sunday, he goes to church. Decides to call his woman out for lunch or some other activity for them to spend quality time together.

That right there, is how he has planned it but let us look at how some of our modern day 'sistas' will change all of that. She is frustrated that she hasn't heard from him like she usually would because he is saying he has been busy. What does she do? She packs a weekend bag and off she goes to 'boo's house' without even letting him know. Tired boo is dragging himself home with his original sleep plan running through his mind. Imagine the look on his face when he sees his woman.

The tendency that many fights will take place in that house is very high and it very likely that our dear lady would leave before her expected date of departure. Some people would argue that she has every right to go to visit her man and spend the weekend with him. Says who?

This man is your boyfriend and not your husband. Ladies, please get it into your heads once and for all that the two do not mix. As your boyfriend, he has every right to do what he wants as he is not answerable to you or anyone else. If he wants to spend twenty-four hours with you, he will and if he says, this week, no show; use the week to do something productive with your own life as well. When he becomes your husband, the story changes and he can report all his moves to you.

I had a friend who spent most of her time at her boyfriend's place. It was so bad that her landlady told her to come and pick her stuff from her own apartment so she could rent the place out to someone else. My friend's reason for being around the man all the time was so she could keep an eye on him. That level of insecurity is both alarming and amusing. So you feel he can't do what he wants to do with you sitting next to him? He's a man and they are smooth in their dealings, so take a chill pill and enjoy the moments you share together.

I sometimes felt bad for the guy because you could see frustration written all over his face but I wondered why he wouldn't just 'man up' and send her to her own house. You don't want to be with someone and the person starts getting seriously irritated by your presence; that is not cool because the love fades rapidly from that point on.

When you are invited, if you have the time, go and have fun; otherwise, please stay in your house. Like I said before, everything is happening so fast these days that we can't even catch our breath so please don't misuse that one day or three hours you have to relax. You owe it to yourself.

CHAPTER TWENTY
GROWING APART

Mary and James were in a stable relationship by all standards: beautiful couple, had good jobs, shared mutual friends, were engaged in some community services and were active members in church.

Weekdays were strictly for work but their offices were close to each other, so, James would always wait to take Mary home before going home himself. During weekends they would be so involved in their extra-curricular activities, that there was barely time for them to really spend together.

Their lives became a very monotonous one with the same routine month after month. Soon, they grew apart not because they didn't love each other but because they didn't realise when the spirit of boredom had taken over and they'd become uninterested in each other.

This happens to many relationships after a while and it is very sad to see or hear that two people gave up on what would have been a great love story, for an excuse as 'lame' as boredom.

Relationships are like plants. The beginning of the relationship is the sowing of the seed. This stage comes with a lot of excitement and hope. The two of you can't wait to see where your journey leads you and it is all good. But then you need to clear unwanted weeds from around your plant, water it and allow enough sunlight to get to it. You constantly keep an eye on it and all that work keeps you interested. That is what should happen in a relationship as well.

You can't just be doing the exact same thing (which in most cases is a big nothing) and expect the fondness, the excitement and tenderness to grow. You need to put in a good dose of work.

Let's get back to the plant, which by this time is flourishing. The leaves are so green and it is a true delight to look at. The person who planted it has a deep satisfaction because his efforts have paid off. The same thing happens with a relationship that you didn't allow to whither. You both are in a great place and the love you share has doubled and it is because you put in the work.

The truth is that it is easier to prevent the growing apart phase than it is to rekindle love when it goes sour. Here are a few steps:

Be an interesting partner. Nothing kills a good mood like dull and boring company. You are supposed to be your craziest, goofiest self with your partner. Let your guard down and feel free. Let them see the fun side of you and if you don't have a fun side, please create it. You cannot be too serious all the time. You are not the only person on earth with stuff to do, places to be and targets to meet.

An old and dear friend once described it as 'rain falling inside one's head' which manifests on the outside. Don't always allow what you are going through inside to ruin the moments you share together. You need each other to relieve the pressure, so please resurrect that dead adventurous spirit in you and have some fun.

Spontaneity is a necessary ingredient for keeping things interesting between couples. Every once in a while, do something outside of the box. A friend's boyfriend had not seen her in two weeks because they had this huge crisis at her workplace which they succeeded in fixing but the young man had had enough. He walked into the building where the lady worked, passed her by, asked for the Manager's office, came out a few minutes later and whisked his woman out of her seat and the building. Nobody knows what he told the Manager to convince him but our dear, young man ended up having both lunch and dinner with his woman.

She tells that story to anyone who cares to listen and they have been married for twelve years. His reaction was over the top but do something you normally wouldn't do every once in a while and you will see the great impact it has on your relationship.

When you feel your relationship is getting stale or losing its fire, please, talk about it with your partner in a gentle way. You don't want to look like a complainant or nag at this point because you would only make a bad situation worse. Discuss your feelings and come up with the best solutions which would make you both happy.

Go down memory lane every now and then. This one is a personal favourite because it worked for me. Some of the things I have written in this book are from my experiences and I take great pride in that fact, because I can use it to impart knowledge.

Anyway, at one point in my relationship, my man and I drifted apart and it got so bad we could barely stand each other. Mistakes were made and lessons learned. We grew up and decided to fight for what we believed in which is us and what we share.

Along the line, I had this wonderful idea to send him what I call my 'special' text messages which he has become obsessed with, by the way. In them, I would discuss my day, my life, his life, our lives and he started seeing things from my point of view and it felt like we were discovering each other all over again.

I would also bring up memories from when we started our

journey because I know as a man, he would most likely have forgotten some of those things. This single act was a game changer for us. It was our bonding moment and we both looked forward to me sending and him reading the texts.

Find a way to bring back cherished memories because it not only keeps them alive but has the magical power of rekindling the love that was there the first time they happened.

Don't allow your love life to grow stale and boring. Cultivate it with care and watch it grow and blossom. You will be happy you did.

CHAPTER TWENTY-ONE
CONFLICT RESOLUTION

There is no society, no friendship and no family where fights don't happen every now and then; we cannot agree on everything all of the time because views and opinions differ.

In relationships, it may be more common because several factors trigger it; the fact that men and women are wired differently for starters, emotional differences and of course mood swings due to hormonal changes to name a couple of differences . Healthy fights are necessary in relationships and anyone who says they don't fight in their relationship should check properly because something is wrong.

Unhealthy fights are the ones where abuse and violence come into the picture and in this case I say, run for your life. No matter how nice and generous an abuser is, your life is way more important; so, help yourself by getting out.

What would two people in a relationship normally fight about?

Who loves who more: this factor is a funny one but quite common. When two people don't know how to communicate their feelings properly, there are bound to be instances where one person believes in their mind that they love the other more. The one who feels he/she loves more starts feeling unappreciated and undervalued. Their next action is to put up an attitude and it is uncomfortable to be around.

Attention: Like I keep saying, life is getting more complex and busier by the day and a person can really forget to keep up with other aspects of their lives. This is not quite understood by their partners however, because their feelings have to be taken into consideration. They want to be given attention when they need it and they feel it is your obligation to give it to them. The whole thing becomes really messed up really fast.

Quality time: You remember that honeymoon phase at the beginning of your relationship, when you would take long walks together, snuggle and binge watch your favourite shows on Netflix or just sit together outdoors, chatting about every and anything? That is gone now, right? And you just want to scratch your partner's eyes out (figuratively) each time he/she shuts down your suggestions for some quality time together.

Over familiarity with members of the opposite sex: Yeah, we get it! You are super cute but that is no passport to flirt with everyone who flashes their teeth to you; all in the name of being nice. It rubs your partner up the wrong way and it is the cause of many fights.

Timing: This one is crucial and it affects those who belong to the category of 'serious' relationship. You know the ones whom in the eyes of everyone else should settle down as man and wife eventually; yes, them. There are too many fights attached to timing because the question of 'where is this relationship going?' becomes the order of the day. They clearly have a good thing going and they are financially capable but it is stuck right there and it becomes a big problem, especially for the woman who feels time is being wasted for no apparent reason.

Now that we have examined some of the reasons people in relationships fight, let us see ways to resolve conflicts so they don't escalate to the point of no return.

Communicate: You cannot put up an attitude because you are frustrated that your partner is not showing you enough love when the person is not even aware of how you feel. He/she is not a magician or psychic to know what is going on with you. The funniest part is that sometimes their partner will ask them why they are acting out and they'll reply, 'no reason'. This doesn't help in anyway so be open and let it all out. Be direct as well; when you start using indirect ways to express yourself, your partner won't quite follow and it becomes irritating.

Choose your battles: You see that particular issue at that particular time, please tackle just that. Don't go bringing what happened two years ago with a slice of what happened seven months back. It only escalates the problem. Tackle one issue at a time and leave it at that. While you are at it, do it tastefully. Don't shoot the entire blame on your partner like a dagger; it doesn't help.

Listen: It is imperative to listen to your partner's complaint. I mean really listen and get where they are coming from. Don't belittle it and don't shrug it off. One thing which really helps is to try and put yourself in your partner's shoes and mentally visualise how you would feel if you were in their place.

Change: It has been said several times that a person would change only for the person they feel they want to change for. I am not saying you should alter your life to please another person but your actions are hurting someone else and it would be good for you to change some of those points they have brought to you as concerns. It guarantees their happiness and your piece of mind.

Don't allow tiny issues and fights to destroy a world of happiness that awaits you; fix it before it becomes too late.

CHAPTER TWENTY-TWO
BABY DADDY/BABY MAMA/ LOVE CHILD

Children are a beautiful and special gift from God. They bring so many well-packaged blessings from Heaven plus they are so cute, you just don't want to stop cuddling them. However, there is a new disheartening trend going on in recent times which entails children being born for the wrong reasons. Let me explain!

The 'husbands are scarce' reason: there's a myth going about that men are suddenly becoming extinct and women have to do everything they possibly can to grab the ones they can grab. What better way to do this than to use the old practice of getting pregnant for them? In their rather shallow minds, that will keep him glued to them forever.

Let's face the truth: you seriously can't believe that trick still works and if you do, I am deeply sorry for you. If you are lucky, he will stick around to bring up the child but when it is time for him to choose a life partner, there's a ninety-eight per cent chance that it won't be you.

The survival of the fittest' reason: this one is similar to the first but in this case, the man is involved with several women and they all know, somehow. Someone succeeds in getting pregnant for the randy man and it is celebration time because she holds the key to being with him for life (I'm just being sarcastic). Stop with the nonsense, please! That kind of man will have children littered all over because he is irresponsible and you really don't matter to him.

The 'money making' reason: these ones are in it strictly for financial gains. They see a good-looking rich, young man, they succeed in getting him close enough, they do everything to get pregnant, he tells them he is not ready to settle down yet, she says it's okay as long as he will take care of the child, he accepts responsibiliy and bingo, she won!

It is important to note that such ladies are in it for material reasons and when I mentioned earlier that she would do anything to get pregnant, I meant even going somewhere else to get the deed done and pinning it on her victim sometimes. Yes, they are that desperate.

The 'love child' reason: in this case, the two people involved are actually in love but still uncertain of where the future would take them. Most of the time, they are quite young and naïve. They go engaging in sexual activities that they are truly not prepared for; then, boom there's a pregnancy.

In some other cases, they are much older but the man in question is married but claims it is his 'side piece' that he is in love with. She ends up getting pregnant and they actually have the baby.

There are so many reasons why babies are born out of wedlock these days but whatever the reason; they are born and they are part of your lives. The questions around this topic in connection to relationships are these: how does your partner feel about your child? How do you balance having a new relationship and taking care of your child? What do you do when your partner cheated on you and had a baby somewhere else? How do you move on when you realise that all you are to him/her is a baby daddy/mummy? How do you handle dating a single dad or mum?

Let's begin with how a new partner would react to the fact that you have a child. In the past, having children out of wedlock was less common because of how much stigma was attached to it but nowadays, people have become more 'liberal'.

This is how to handle this situation; do not let your new partner discover on his or her own that you have a child. The reaction you will get from that may not be a very good one. Tell the person beforehand about the kid and give them the opportunity to mentally prepare to take you and the child as a complete package. Unless the person in question has a serious dislike for kids or is intolerant of certain situations, I don't think it will be much of a problem if you are honest from the beginning.

To you who has decided to be involved with a single father/mother, I have this to say: You will need to acquire two new virtues if you don't have them already: patience and tolerance. The child is the centre of your partner's universe and you cannot change that, so don't even try.

Any resistance you put up will automatically push you out the door. You are not going to compete with the child for your partner's attention. Don't be too quick to want the child to accept and like you, so you go about doing ridiculous and unnecessary things. Let it happen gradually and naturally.

It's a child for heaven's sake and they easily fall in love with genuine people and when they do, they will help to solidify your relationship with their parent.

Balancing a new relationship and the attention you give your child is no easy feat on any level but it can be done. If you are a woman, you have to make sure you take good care of your child and you don't shift the attention from him/her in any way. If you do, the child immediately starts resenting your new man because he is the distraction and you can't win.

Don't just push the man onto your child immediately. It has to be done gradually and with care. Let the child get comfortable with him visiting once in a while before he becomes a more frequent presence in both of your lives.

If you are a man, the same rule applies but yours is a bit trickier because both women and children require a lot of attention. Try not to miss any important dates with your woman, play dates with your child, school activities and meal times. You can do this easily but don't allow it to put too much pressure on you. When you cannot make an appointment, explain nicely to the one you are about to disappoint so they don't go getting any wrong ideas.

So, you have had a child and there's no marriage prospect or future plans in the person's agenda which includes you; heartbreaking I understand but it is what it is, so time to buckle up.

First of all, you have been blessed with that beautiful child that God has decorated your life with so be grateful to Him every second of every day. Next, you have to realise that no matter what you receive as support, the child is your responsibility. Baby mama/daddy is not a heavyweight title so it won't pay you. Get your life together and get a job. If you can't get a job, start a business, no matter how small. You cannot afford to relax at this point, so get to work.

While you are at it, you have to realise that you are human and deserve to be loved properly. If someone is interested in giving you the love you deserve, don't hold back as long as you have checked it out and it will be good for you and the child. Don't make the mistake of spending years waiting for someone who has made it clear that he/she doesn't want anything to do with you.

You have been in a relationship with someone and all of a sudden, the person gets someone else pregnant or gets pregnant for someone else. This has got to be one of the most painful phenomena on earth. It takes a lot to keep breathing normally after it hits you. Your world is shattered in a flash but you will survive it, trust me. Men are less forgiving in situations like these. They wouldn't even want to see the face of the woman who betrayed him like that. Women on the other hand will hate you fast and curse the day you came into their lives but they are generally more forgiving.

The real test here is how much strength you will need to make certain decisions after you have made the big discovery that there's a baby by someone else. It takes a great deal of strength and you will need to channel Heaven because only God can lead you towards the right path.

If the man intentionally, unapologetically and unremorsefully hurt you in this way; I say leave him and move on. If it was a drunken mistake or a sober mistake and you know your man will not intentionally hurt you like that and you see how it affects him more than you, then forgive him. If you think you can go on with the relationship, then you have to tap into your inner strength again, because every time you see the child will be a reminder of what happened. Time, however, heals most of the wounds; so please be patient.

Remember, the child is not to be blamed in any way so don't take it out on him/her. Most baby mamas in this situation are the main problem because they come with a lot of drama. You, the man in this whole fiasco, have a lot of work to do.

Firstly, make sure the child is yours. There is nothing as painful as spending time and money in bringing up a child and you later discover the child isn't yours. The wisest thing to do at this point is to take the test and rule out any deception.

When you have confirmed the paternity of the child, it is

time to lay ground rules. Make it clear to the baby mama that there will be nothing between you two except the support and care of the child. Let her know how much you love your woman and demand that she respects your relationship.

Then, let your woman know as well that there is nothing between you and your baby mama and beg your woman to accept the child. Don't force the situation but handle it with extreme care.

Time will take care of healing every other wound. Don't be too quick to give up on a good thing because of a mistake or bad situation. If you are strong enough to carry it then go ahead and don't listen to anyone because you wear the shoes and know where they pinch. Always remember that God will never give you what you can't handle.

If you are unsure of your purpose here on earth, if you are still too much of a child yourself, if you are afraid of responsibility, please don't go bringing an innocent child into your confused world. If it happens, make sure you will do what is best for the child, what is best for the people in your life and what is best for you.

CHAPTER TWENTY-THREE
FAMILY INFLUENCE

When two people start a relationship, according to the norms; it is strictly their business and others should do well to stay out of it unless they have been invited in. That doesn't quite work in Africa; I can tell you as a proud African.

Family and friends have a lot of influence on a relationship here and I would only talk about what I am conversant with. Since we had already discussed friends in chapter eighteen, we should also focus on the kind of influence family has on relationships.

Family as the 'matchmaker': there have been uncountable cases where relationships have been born from the matchmaking savvy of family members. Mothers linking their sons with girls they felt will make the perfect partners for them. Fathers who link up their children to extend their old-time friendship to another generation. Sisters linking their friends with their brothers and vice versa. These things happen all the time. Do some of them succeed? Sure. Do most of them fail? Absolutely.

I am a firm believer in someone going to some place and out of the blue, meeting another person they really like, under their own conditions. It gives the relationship a different vibe because there was something about the person which called out to you.

The whole matchmaking idea doesn't really sit well with me. No one can know you more than you know yourself but your family has spent enough time with you to be able to ascertain that someone might be just right for you, in cases where you find it difficult to get that special person on your own.

You may be a very shy person who can't approach a lady on your own. You may be a bad judge of character who keeps falling for the wrong kind of women or you may be the kind of lady who finds it hard to go out and mingle but really wants to have the right man in her life. Well, whatever the reason, you need help and who better to render that help but people who know you well enough: family.

The only issue I have is when they go about imposing partners on a person without being asked. I find it really annoying and I am just a bystander, so I can imagine what the victim in question would be going through. Don't let yourself be intimidated or pushed around to please your family; it is your life and your love story so stick to what makes you happy.

Family as the 'determining factor': you have gone out to the jungle, fought all the odds and found yourself a wonderful woman/man. You decide to introduce this person to your family; because they are a part of you on one hand and you are serious about the relationship on the other.

Lo and behold, they set their eyes on your partner and object woefully. It is a very nerve-wracking situation because you love both parties and want them to love each other as well. You would have to check your family's reason for objecting so much. They may be valid reasons but if they are not; handle it with utmost maturity and express your feelings calmly to your family.

Family as the 'middle-man': when your family loves your partner, they take up several roles in the relationship. They obviously like the two of you together and they will do everything to calm the waters when they suspect the boat is rocking too much (figuratively). In other words, they will act as peacemakers when there is trouble between you and your partner.

They encourage the relationship by showing undying support and any relationship with family backing has a good foundation.

The ugly side of this picture is when the family's interference level is too high. There has to be a balance so that you and your partner would have a say in how your relationship runs.

Someone once asked me how soon is too soon to introduce your partner to your family. This is a huge dilemma for many people because they are either afraid to do it too soon, thereby not giving their family and partner ample time to prepare for the meeting and doing it too late, when it becomes disrespectful to both parties because it has taken too long to happen.

I say: do it when you are comfortable in the relationship. That moment when your heart tells you that he/she is the special one you have been looking for. When you have exhausted the 'getting to know each other' phase is the comfortable place I am talking about and the right time to introduce your man/woman to family.

The reason is simple. You don't want a scenario where you introduce them both and they like each other and you realise that he/she wasn't really what you thought you had found. Then you have to break everyone up. It's very messy and makes you look irresponsible.

The best thing to do would be to talk about your man/woman with your family before introducing them. Tell them nice things about this person, tell them what you like and dislike about this person and let them paint a mental picture first. This would help a great deal in smoothing the journey and calming the nervousness on all sides.

CHAPTER TWENTY-FOUR
THE POWER OF APPRECIATION

Have you ever shown someone some random act of kindness and they just turnaround and walk away without as much as a 'thank you'? I bet you wish you had control over time so you could take it all back, because that person didn't deserve it. On the flip side, when you do get that 'thank you' with a smile as topping, it is an extraordinary feeling and that is the power of appreciation.

I still don't understand where people get their feeling of entitlement these days. They walk around feeling like they deserve everything you do for them. Why shouldn't they? After all, they are doing you a favour by being in your life. (Load of crap).

I have sat for long hours wondering and I think I finally cracked it. They feel so entitled because we let them. We will get to that in a moment but first; let us examine the effects a good dose of appreciation has on an individual in a relationship.

First of all, you asked for help and you were given it. You were in a fix and didn't know where else to turn but the man/woman in your life stepped up and selflessly rendered the help you so desperately needed. Then you turn around and belittle that, by carrying on as if they did nothing. Wow! Really? It is despicable to say the least.

Men are fond of committing this atrocity. Some men, I mean, will treat a woman like she has half a brain and whatever a woman does for them is their right and privilege. She did it because she loves you and you were probably looking pathetic in your helpless state. A woman who loves you will not be okay if you are not okay. That is how a woman operates. You owe her a heartfelt thank you. You should let her know in any way you can, that you appreciate her.

Before the men come for my neck, there are some ladies out there who give us women a bad name as well. I have heard stories from men who bent over backwards to render some help or do something really phenomenal for their women but received a lot of ingratitude and spite in return. That is so not fair.

Secondly, you may not have asked for help but your partner noticed that you needed something and went out of their way to do it for you; even that is not enough in your eyes. You may be upset or you had a lousy day at work; you may be mad at your partner for something else they may have done but do not let those things stop you from noticing nice, helpful and romantic gestures.

Let me tell you what a lack of appreciation would do to you as a couple: it will bring misery. You may or may not ever know how horrible a person feels when their kindness is undervalued. It is like a kick in the abdomen (figuratively). It makes him/her feel very miserable and inadequate. Trust me, you really don't want to be responsible for anyone feeling that way.

When a person keeps doing something over and over again and doesn't get any kind of credit for it, what do you think will happen? Exactly, they would lose interest really fast.

To put the spark into your relationship when it hits rock bottom is hard work, I keep saying, so save yourselves the stress and unhappiness by saying something as simple as thank you.

I mentioned earlier that some people feel entitled to your showing them love, care, generosity and kindness and that is due to the fact that we let them. You should never allow anyone to make you feel like they are doing you a favour by being in your life.

They came to you because they saw something in you that they really liked and it was your choice to say yes or no, as to whether you wanted to embark on that journey with them and you decided to actually do it. Stop giving people reasons to think you have zero value for yourself by allowing them to treat you the way they do.

If you do something today, tomorrow and the next day and don't get good feedback from your partner, talk to him/her about it. If you still don't get good feedback after that, stop doing those things. Learn to say NO. It is not an abomination or a taboo. No one will blame you for saving your dignity.

It is high time we stopped doing too much because, 'oh, I have to do it, if not he will leave me' or 'oh, if I don't do this, she will feel bad and not talk to me again'. Let them go or let them not talk to you; there are worse things in life. They will realise sooner rather than later that they have been going about things in the wrong way and will come back to their senses.

Now for those who still don't grasp how to show appreciation, let me walk you through it.

Just say thank you each time you are given something, taken somewhere or something is done for you. Two words is all it takes. It doesn't just warm the heart of the person but it also motivates that person to do more for you.

Reciprocate when you can. Don't be that person who always says thank you in life. It's not a very good look on you. Whatever you get, try to give back as well. If the person is there for you whenever you need help, try and be there for that person too. It would not only make him/her happy but you, as the giver, as well.

Gifts and gestures matter a lot. A little thank you gift here and there is a necessity for a healthy relationship. I didn't say you should go close your account to buy an appreciation present for your man/woman. That pair of earrings you feel she will like or that beautiful tie you know will match his favourite shirt will do the trick.

If you can't afford all of that, gestures are equally heart-warming. She gets home as a nurse after a hard day's work and you massage her feet or cook her favourite meal. You go to his place and due to his busy schedule, the place is in disarray but by the time he gets back, you have given his house a perfect makeover. Little things like these are the gestures I am talking about.

By now, I am hopeful that you get the picture. Appreciation is the fuel any relationship needs to survive or the fire will quickly burn out, I promise you. It is not expensive though but the goodies you reap from it cannot measure up to all the gold in the world.

CHAPTER TWENTY-FIVE
INTIMACY

I am almost a hundred per cent sure that some people reading this book to this point have wondered why I didn't discuss sex as a topic; well, I won't. You are an adult and I am sure you have had enough sex education classes to last you a lifetime and there are unlimited copies of books and websites where you can get all the additional information you feel you are lacking.

The topic of sex these days nauseates me, as people have taken it way out of its original intent and made it extremely cheap and degrading. There is something more powerful and meaningful than sex in a relationship and that is intimacy and people have not grasped its intensity yet. Let's try to fix that, shall we?

There are various definitions of intimacy but one really struck me as very simple and concise; intimacy means deeply knowing another person and feeling deeply known. That, ladies and gentlemen is the sum of it! To say you are truly intimate with someone, there has to be a deep, emotional connection but there exist four types of intimacy.

There is physical intimacy and this type has to do with being present at a particular place and time. You need to spend quality time together and it can't be overemphasised. These are the moments you get to see the other person's reactions to certain things; you get to observe some of their habits; you get to have fun and laugh. There is magic when two people in love spend quality time together, because they form a strong bond and friendship in the process.

There is emotional intimacy which entails connecting on a deep emotional level. This is where you are both honest about your true feelings. The person in your life gets to understand exactly how you operate emotionally and it helps because when a person knows and understands how you operate emotionally, they can easily catch up with you. You two can be your most vulnerable selves with ease.

A friend of mine told me that she and her man had issues which nearly separated them but in the course of repairing it, one evening, he got so emotional that he started crying. She, on the other hand had never had a man cry over her before and it shocked her. She came to me, complaining that she didn't feel it was very manly of him. I laughed at first but I made her understand that her man was at his most vulnerable state with her and in his mind, she is the one person he would allow to see him in that state, because of the intimacy he felt they shared. So, instead of being shocked, I asked her to relish it and be her true self with him as well.

Let your partner in; don't hold back on your feelings. It unlocks doors in your relationship that you never even knew were shut. Connecting on an emotional level is more powerful than any of us can ever imagine.

There is also the sensual intimacy which entails physicality. You get to connect by holding hands, hugging, kissing and caressing. This has nothing to do with sex but the feeling of understanding how your body responds to your partner's touch. Women, in particular, love sensual intimacy because they feel pampered by their man and they enjoy the connection they both feel at this point.

Then, there's sexual intimacy. Now, you understand that sex is not intimacy but a part of it. Sex is the act of having intercourse and it has its own power and magic when it is the right time and place.

It is important to note that every couple has a different level of appreciation of these types of intimacy. What works for one couple may not necessarily work for another, so you have the assignment to know which one it is that speaks to the two of you and build on it.

How do we build intimacy? I will tell you, of course.

Firstly, be open and honest with each other. You will get it completely wrong if you hide things or are sneaky. Let there be trust between you two and you need to feel free to talk about whatever. Who else do you want to be yourself with if not your partner?

Secondly, please be present and in the moment when you two are together. Don't start daydreaming when he is talking about his feelings and don't think about your unreached target in the office when she is pouring her heart out to you. Be present. Look into each other's eyes, smile as much as possible, flirt and be playful.

Learn to be understanding and accepting of your partner and while you are at it, accept yourself too. The two of you are different and have flaws as well as fragments but don't go all judgmental. It only brings tension and negativity and that is far from our aim.

I said spend quality time together but it doesn't mean you should follow him/her around like a puppy. Give each other time to take you in and enjoy memories you have already created together. Give time for the other person to miss you a little.

Bear in mind that it doesn't happen overnight. Intimacy is something which will take a while to build. I speak not only from theory but from experience when I tell you that, if you do things right and what you share is true, the intimacy you both will enjoy is the most surreal experience there is.

CHAPTER TWENTY-SIX
MATCHMAKING/ONLINE DATING/BLIND DATES

If you have been reading this book from the beginning, like I think you have, you must have seen where I mentioned that I am not a big fan of matchmaking.

I tried online dating once and it didn't quite work out. I went on two blind dates which happened to be total disasters. However, I am also a believer in not letting a bad experience or two stop me from encouraging someone else, if it would help the person.

Matchmaking in my understanding is when someone or a group of people decide to link up two people they feel would be great for each other. The confidence they have is from having been around the two people in question enough, to know that their personalities would make a great union.

In life, we need helpers in most situations as we cannot do many things on our own and if you have tried something several times and failed at it several times, you would agree with me that you really need help. I may not like matchmaking but it has worked for many people. However, there are some ground rules:

To begin with, it is about you and not pleasing anyone else. If you are not comfortable with the whole idea, don't do it. The intentions may be good but the life is yours.

Secondly, draw your own conclusions upon meeting this person. Just because your mum said it, or your aunt knows him from when she was a teacher in kindergarten, or your sister said she works in the same office with the lady doesn't mean they know enough to determine whether this person is right for you or not. Draw your own conclusions about this person and if you feel it doesn't click, then call it off.

Thirdly, you need to be very observant when you are around this person because you need to match the things you see in front of you, to all the details you have been given beforehand.

Don't go smiling aimlessly at him because he can't stop flashing his wonderful set of teeth at you or staring at her like you can't breathe, because she has an awesome figure. Look beyond that and if everything checks out, you can feel free to continue on your love journey.

Don't only rely on information given to you by the matchmaker but try and do a little digging of your own once you have decided that he/she is a promising candidate. There's nothing like being too careful; given that we can never be too sure about people these days.

To my dear online daters, I have this to say; be very careful! In your case, you are involved with someone you can only see through a screen and talk to over a phone. Generally, what they tell you is what you take as true until the situation proves otherwise. There are so many people who started by dating online and are happily married today and it could be you. The fact that many fake and unstable people fill up dating sites, doesn't mean there no love-hungry people like yourself in there as well.

Don't go throwing yourself into crazy dating sites. Find out which ones are good and promising. When you do find one, go through as many profiles as you can; don't latch on to the first person who catches your fancy because they might not be it. Have a few choices and keep narrowing it down 'til you get the one you feel is just about right.

Let the other person disclose more about him/herself than you, to enable you get the gist of how their head functions before you go in fully. Don't go giving too much information too soon because you won't be able to retrieve it later if things don't work out and you would have let a stranger too far into your business.

In today's world of video calls and FaceTime, please try as much as possible to be your natural authentic self. Let the person fall in love with the real you. Don't always 'glam up' because he/she would live with the real you eventually, if things work out. And be very honest too; you don't want to meet the person and they discover that half the things you told them were lies.

This one has been said over and over again and people don't listen. When you two decide to meet for the first time, always do it in a public place. More for security reasons than personal. Plus, there's less tension due to distractions from other people around and it can help you relax better and ease into the first date.

You have spent months chatting and describing yourselves and talking about your likes, dislikes and hobbies and all of the personal data; so, meeting for the first time is not the time to start all of that again. This is a time to be relaxed and enjoy each other's presence and be a little touchy-feely if you are both comfortable with that.

Now, blind dates are products of matchmaking because someone has to set the date up for the two people in most cases. You are going in there not knowing what the person looks like and not knowing what to expect and it is a very nerve-wracking experience, to say the least.

The one thing to keep in mind when you are going on a blind date is to be open-minded. You may likely see the opposite of what you expected but just be ready to take it in. Dress simply, decently, appropriately and classy. Don't give away too much but don't make them feel you didn't try enough.

No matter how much you disapprove of your date, do not make the mistake of letting it show. Be kind and courteous. The other person is a human being with feelings and you don't want to hurt them. He/she is most likely as nervous as you are and that might make them misbehave at first. Trust me, blind dates can be truly awkward, so try as much as possible to fight the urge to make it more so.

Dating used to be way simpler back in the day but today, there is variety and we all know it's the spice of life. Whichever form of dating you find yourself in, dear reader, make the most of it, because you never know how the first page of your love story was destined to begin. Be open-minded but careful at the same time and have fun while at it.

CHAPTER TWENTY-SEVEN
ABUSE

Abuse is horrible! It is one of the scariest things to go through as a person and leaves a big scar after the person has successfully got out of it. What is abuse? It is simply the act of someone constantly using power and fear to control another person.

Abusers have a tendency to manipulate their victims into seeing them as their lord and master, so it becomes easier to prey on them.

There are various forms of abuse in relationships; some people going through some of these forms of abuse are actually ignorant of the fact that they are being abused, which makes the situation a lot more critical and dangerous. Some others have become so used to being treated in such terrible ways, that they would rather remain there than get out. Let's examine these forms of abuse:

Physical abuse: in this case there is bodily contact involved and the abuser intentionally inflicts physical pain and injury on his/her victim. Some examples are biting, punching, kicking, pulling your hair, throwing things at you, grabbing, pushing and pulling.

Listen to me; you need to get out of this kind of situation because it will only get more violent as time goes on. I have heard of women in relationships who claim they like it when some force is used on them or they are beaten up once in a while. Clearly, you need psychological evaluation because something is definitely wrong with you. Get out before you lose something as

described forms of abuse, put a stop to it by getting out. Remember, you are in the relationship stage and marriage will only amplify what you think is bad now.

To those in physically abusive relationships, get out and report to the right authorities as soon as possible.

To those in emotionally abusive relationships, kick the abuser out of your life without delay because you are way stronger than their twisted minds can ever conceive.

To the sexually abused, please report the beast to the police or other relevant authority, so that they can at least pay a little for what they have put you through. Talk to someone about it, even if you would feel ashamed. It is not your fault and you are not alone.

To the financially abused, I say, don't give them that kind of power over you. Look for something to do for yourself no matter how little and be your own person. That is the best form of revenge against your abuser. Also, learn to say no when they come for your money because it is yours. Be strong!

To the digitally abused, have you heard of something called 'blocking'? Find that button and use it without delay, because you have the power to do so and you deserve your peace of mind.

CHAPTER TWENTY-EIGHT
MONEY TALK

Money makes the world go round. Money answereth all things. Money is the root of all evil. There are so many of these sayings and we have heard them time and time again.

Money is good. It solves problems, takes you places, gives you great opportunities, broadens your horizon, gives you comfort and makes you glitter. On the flip side, the excessive love and pursuit of money can destroy you in ways you never imagined.

In relationships, issues related to money are seldom discussed and I have always wondered whether it is because the topic is not as spicy as people like or they just want to avoid it because it sounds complex.

Whatever the reason, I will try to make it interesting for anyone reading because these are issues which impede the growth and sustenance of what would have been a great relationship.

I will begin by explaining what money or having money means to a man. Every man is a born provider unless he is naturally selfish or stingy. Men are wired to work and provide for themselves and anyone in their lives. A man has set goals from when he is much younger and when he is not able to achieve some of those goals at a certain age, you can see the frustration written all over him.

A man feels he is valued more with the things he has accomplished in life and we can't change that, no matter how hard we try. That is why you see some men at an age where you, the onlooker, feels he should be in a meaningful relationship or even married but in his mind, he just can't; because he feels he hasn't reached the point where he can comfortably bring someone else into his life and make that person truly happy.

Nothing kills a man like when a loved one really needs something from him and he is incapable of providing that need. Ladies, please understand this fact because it's a game changer. Don't go berating a man at this point for not granting your wishes, because he already feels horrible on his own.

What does money mean to women? Money just means being able to satisfy her needs at a particular time. The needs vary of course; she may be craving a particular dish, may want to take a trip, want to buy that dress, to buy those shoes which match the handbag she bought a while back.

A woman is a natural manager. She has the ability to take something and break it down to last longer and satisfy everyone. That is how women are wired. Well, unless she is very materialistic and unreasonable.

Here are some pointers to help people figure out their way when it comes to money matters in a relationship and I will mix them up a little.

Dear man, I understand how important it is to you to make money. I applaud your seen and unseen efforts and I pray that Heaven blesses your hard work but please remember, that is not all there is to life.

You don't want to work your whole life and when you feel you have become successful, you realise that you missed out on the simple and beautiful things in life like love, marriage, kids and good health. All that money won't be worth it at that point.

You need to understand that God is the only person in

control of your destiny and before you were born, He had mapped out the course of your life. You are in no competition with anyone and you don't need to do too much to impress anybody. Take your time and relax as much as possible.

Remember, you have no control of time and your speed will only lead you to quick exhaustion and you will eventually crash. Yes, there's pressure on you but you need to take life easy.

Dear woman, you are to be taken care of as the beautiful delicate flower you are. You are supposed to be maintained and polished so that you continue to glitter. All of that is acceptable but it doesn't mean you should forget that you can be productive as well. Stop giving millions of excuses about you not going to school or not getting a job; you have a talent, so develop it and make your own money.

Let me give you an important tip which I'm sure you have noticed but just chose to ignore. Men, these days, find a hardworking woman very attractive. No man is interested in a woman who has turned herself into a modern day 'tax collector'. You just want this person to give to you and for that person to take care of you. It is not right.

The world we live in has become more complex as I have mentioned repeatedly and you can't afford to depend on anyone entirely; so get busy. Besides, no money is as sweet as the one you made yourself.

Dear man, it is true that you have found a hardworking, independent woman but please don't sit in your corner and assume that she doesn't need a gift or a trip once in a while. Surprise her every now and then. She will feel that truly, you have her interest at heart and you do care about her welfare. She will most likely treasure those gifts more than anything else. You, the man, will feel gratified as well because you did something nice for your woman.

Another thing you should stop doing is to let your woman always come asking for one thing or another. Trust me, it's not easy for her to do that. Let it always ring in your head that as a woman, she will always need something. Don't go assuming that she's fine.

Dear woman, you are not a beggar. You want everything under the skies. You spend time going through all the shops online and your taste is unreasonably high. On your own, you won't spend that kind of money if you were the one making it; so why do you want to kill someone's son? Reduce your high demands and focus on more meaningful goals.

Dear man, some women are very high maintenance naturally, so you need to check yourself and your capabilities. If you know you cannot handle her taste, please do not venture. Stay within your range. I know you like what you see when you look at her but it may have taken her a lot of time, effort and money to get to that point. Admire and move on. Stop increasing the amount of pressure you already have in your life by reaching out for things you can't afford.

Money is great, dear reader! Relationships are sweet when there is comfort and you both have peace of mind. However, stay within your range to avoid bringing unnecessary strain on your union. Communicate your feelings if you don't like how your partner handles money. Remember that money doesn't buy happiness at all. Your happiness depends on how you live your life and the choices you make.

CHAPTER TWENTY-NINE
TOXIC RELATIONSHIPS

When you pick up a container and see the word 'toxic' written on it, what is the first thing you think of? You got that right: it is harmful. The next reaction is to keep that container away from you and anyone else it may harm. The same applies to toxic relationships; they harm you in ways you may or may not be conscious of.

It is important to note that there is a difference between being in a toxic relationship and being in an abusive relationship. In an abusive relationship (refer to chapter twenty-seven), dangerous and harmful acts are performed on an individual, like battery or rape but with toxic relationships, the individual harms him or herself by refusing to get out of a situation which is clearly unhealthy for them.

When you are in a healthy relationship, you feel safe, warm, respected, an ability to share control and take decisions but for those in a toxic relationship, the feeling of insecurity, control, disrespect and dominance are the order of the day.

Let's examine some of the characteristics of a toxic relationship to shed more light on the topic for better understanding.

In a toxic relationship, you give way more than you receive. You are always ready to do your partner's bidding no matter the time or how convenient it is; you remember the things which matter to him or her and are sure to help out in any way you possibly can. You give your love, you give your energy, you give care and you give your time but you never get anything in return.

In a toxic relationship, there is a constant feeling of unhappiness. Who in their right minds can be happy in a situation where they are treated like 'slaves'. Funnily enough, I have seen a few people I know who were in toxic relationships but they were always so cheerful and had this huge smile plastered on their faces. If you didn't know their story, you would never have guessed how unhappy they truly were. They are usually very good at pretending that all is well.

There is a lot of hostility in a toxic relationship because the selfish and controlling partner doesn't really care about his/her partner's feelings. They talk to them in harsh and condescending tones and they don't care if they are in public or not.

Due to their insecurities, there is a high level of mistrust in a toxic relationship. No matter how much the truth looks them in the eye, they just don't believe it is the truth. That is why you see them always calling to find out their partner's exact location, always checking phones, always issuing warnings against people their partner talks to or mingles with.

There is a high level of disrespect. Your feelings don't matter and in their minds, they believe that you are incapable of leaving them; so they can afford to do whatever they want. They may go as far as flaunting other people they are seeing in your face, just so you know they can. It makes them feel powerful. They don't just stop at disrespecting you but allow other people to disrespect you as well.

There is a lack of communication. You, on the receiving end, are the one constantly calling and texting to check on them. You try to talk to them but most times, they shut you out. They are just not interested.

There is a never-ending drama in toxic relationships. It is

always one thing or the other and most times it doesn't make sense and shouldn't be an issue but because one person is self-absorbed and controlling and doesn't see any good in what his/her partner does and the other is delusional and weak and can't stand up for him/herself, the drama just continues.

There is a feeling of unworthiness on the receiver in a toxic relationship. Which, by the way, is quite normal if you ask me. Why wouldn't a person feel unworthy when their feelings are trampled upon and they are treated horribly?

Toxic relationships bring out the worst in a person. You look at yourself when you finally succeed in coming out of it and you don't quite recognise the person you have become. It is a very scary experience.

Toxic relationships leave you feeling drained. You have worked and worked and worked to keep the relationship going. You have gone to lengths no other person will understand, because you held on to the hope that one day it will be all right. News flash: it only ends up burning you out.

Picture this scenario: you are climbing a flight of stairs and each time you look up, you can almost swear you see the end but when you get to what seems to be that end, a new flight of stairs appears and it leaves you completely exhausted. Do you understand now?

The question on peoples' minds usually is: why don't they just leave? The bitter truth is that they can't. They have become accustomed to being treated that way and they feel it is normal.

They can't, because as sick as it sounds, they actually love their evil partner and believe that one day, they would change.

They can't because they do not see an escape route and in most cases, they just refuse to see the escape route.

After reading this and identifying that you are in a toxic

relationship; I need you to listen to me! You are too worthy to be treated that way by the bully you call a partner. He/she knows how worthy you truly are and it scares them because they really can't handle your awesomeness. What do they do? They slowly break you down until they have you completely under their control. Get out now!

The right person is just around the corner and he/she is waiting for you. That person will respect you, treasure you, will be there for you in all seasons, will listen when you talk, will be proud to show you off to other people, will respect and love you, will bring out the best in you and will give you reasons to smile every day.

If you don't find that person, it's all good because it will give you time to focus on rebuilding yourself and living your best life.

The weapons you possess to fight a toxic relationship are: choosing your happiness and knowing you are strong enough to get up and get out. Choose to keep that toxic container and its contents away from you today!

CHAPTER THIRTY
JEALOUSY/POSSESSIVENESS

Have you ever been out with your man and you both bump into another lady you know has a serious crush on him? To make matters worse, you see your man responding so charmingly to her greetings and smiles. Yeah, I know! You just feel like pouring the next bowl of water you see around you all over her.

Or, have you been with your group of friends and your woman passes by and one of your friends can't stop gushing over how beautiful your woman is? It's a good thing that they find her so attractive but you just can't help the urge to punch him in the face.

Don't worry, dear reader; I'm not in any way promoting violence. I'm just bringing out into the open, some of your secret wishes in situations like the aforementioned.

Jealousy in tiny doses is actually cute because you see the visible representation of how much your partner values you and wants you all to themselves. It becomes dangerous and sometimes lethal when the jealous partner can no longer control the feeling of jealousy and their reactions to it.

In every relationship, there is supposed to be trust; otherwise, I have no idea what business the two of you have being together. You should be able to go away on a trip or even spend time apart and be sure that your partner will not likely do anything to destroy your flourishing relationship.

I had a friend whose level of distrust for her man was so high that she would wake up in the middle of night in panic because she had a 'feeling' he was cheating on her at that exact moment. You can't completely blame her, after all, he had cheated on her several times; but that is no life and you don't have to ever get to that pathetic point.

When you don't trust your man/woman, it is so easy for jealousy, aka the green-eyed monster to strike your relationship and break it down to tiny pieces. You need to change that mindset you have always had; that your partner has no right to get attracted to other people.

Unless you are involved with a robot, I tell you, it is quite natural for any individual to feel some level of attraction for another person but the way this attraction is handled is what makes the difference.

I know a couple who have devised the brilliant method of turning it into a huge joke when one partner knows that the other finds some other person a tad attractive. They laugh about it but it is simply because they have communicated their feelings so well, that they both know they are not ready to compromise their beautiful relationship for anything and anyone else.

They laugh about it and it's gone. I'm not saying the same should apply to every relationship but find a way to communicate better and maintain trust to avoid unnecessary jealous attacks.

Some experts have tagged jealous people as insecure, fearful people with low self-esteem but I say, anybody can get jealous at any time. Unless you have Othello syndrome or some other form of unhealthy jealous tendencies, it is just a momentary act.

When the person is exposed to more situations where they feel things have gone out of control, then they become afraid that they may lose the person they love; they become insecure because they don't know what may happen next and their self-esteem reduces because they start second-guessing themselves.

It is the assignment of their partners to avoid putting them in situations where this jealousy arises and to always do their best to reassure them when doubts creep in.

If she doesn't like the way you compliment other women, stop it, because there is a high tendency that you don't compliment her that much. If he hates you wearing that mini skirt because of how men gawk at you when you do, stop it. You alone have the power to steer the ship of your relationship the way you expect it to go, so get on with it.

There are many people who confuse jealousy with possessiveness. Possessiveness is the deep need to hold on to someone else for yourself alone. You don't want to share any of that person with someone else. You want to be the only person they think about. You want to be the only one they spend their time with. You have a deep satisfaction knowing that you are in that person's life and he/she is in yours.

Most people have interpreted possessiveness as an obvious sign of love and I might even say it comes with a huge dose of cuteness; but it could become scary and disturbing when it goes wrong.

Listen! You need to be happy with the fact that you have a great relationship going on and you were both lucky to find each other and find what you had been looking for all your lives in this one person. You don't need to go about marking your territory like one of the animals in the jungle because it is unnecessary.

It is good when you show your possessive side once in a while; it actually makes your partner very happy and reassured that you want them all to yourself at all times but leave it at the cute stage, please!

CHAPTER THIRTY-ONE
PATIENCE

Ever heard the expression 'Rome was not built in a day'? Well, nothing good comes easy or fast; otherwise, it would be too good to be true. You need to continue building and working to achieve the kind of results you hoped and prayed for.

That is how successful businesses start as well. I have watched too many interviews and read books about successful business owners and they always say the same thing, 'I started small and put in a lot of work'. The same applies to successful marriages which began with successful relationships.

The world is full of people who specialise in having opinions about other people's relationships when some of them don't even have one and for those who are in relationships, they don't even understand their own journey; so, you begin to wonder how they can dish out advice to others. You will have to learn to run your race with guidance from God alone.

Always remember that your partner is another individual and he/she is not perfect. They have brought as much baggage to the relationship as you have or maybe more. If you can't handle it and you realise this fact on time, please get out whilst it's still early.

Don't hold on to something which brings you any suffering of any kind when you have an alternative. However, if you know your love for your partner is strong enough to weather any storm, then you need to be patient.

Your partner may have some attitudinal problems which

they may not even be aware of and all their lives, no one has been able to point these things out to them. Instead of berating them at every chance you have, be patient and gradually draw their attention to those things you find repulsive or annoying.

Get ready to face a lot of resistance and defiance from them; face it, no one likes being told the truth about them at first but with time, it will sink in. The fact that they do things you don't like is no reason for you to misbehave as well. Oh, she nags too much so let's find another girl who will be more submissive. No! That only exposes your own immaturity. If you truly love him/her, you will put in work.

Now, ladies, I need you to listen to me because this one is specifically for you. I know you have had fantasies about the kind of man you would love to meet and have in your life and he will come but it may not be what you fantasised about.

Some of our men grew up not really understanding what a true relationship is supposed to feel or look like and it is not taught in schools so they have had zero guidance until they met you.

Women are naturally more emotional and we pick on things whilst growing up because we would read novels, watch movies and replay love songs that we love. Men were not structured to do those things because they were considered unmanly so they based their knowledge on their relationship with the opposite sex on their raw animal needs, which are mostly physical.

Due to the above facts, you need to become a teacher when you notice that you have a willing student. Bear in mind that you can't force a man to love you properly, especially when the love is not true. He has to make himself available to be taught and directed because he genuinely loves you and is ready to make the relationship work. Do not bombard him; instead, take things slowly and patiently win him over.

My dear reader, relationships are not for the weak-hearted or the immature because the tests and challenges which will hit you back-to-back will leave you in complete shock, if you do not possess inner strength and wisdom from above.

I'm sure many of you understand exactly what I mean; you get into this thing and the beginning is like a fairytale. All is sugar and spice and everything nice with the incessant calls, sweet messages, long romantic walks and flirty stares; then it gets real and quickly, too. The 'honeymoon' stage is over and it feels like things have settled.

You are just getting used to the new normal when it turns around and gets ugly; you feel like you don't even have a minute to catch your breath. It's one thing after another and after another and you want to scream. The tendency is for you to call it quits at this point but don't do it, if you think the situation is not completely hopeless.

People will tell you to leave after you have told them what you are going through but here is something smart that I heard from a documentary on relationships I watched. It says, 'Don't listen to advice from people who won't understand the way you love.' Yes, oh yes! You alone know your love language, your love system, your love strategy and your love journey.

Listen to what your heart tells you because it will always speak. Relationships are a battlefield and everyone is fighting their battles, so you won't let anyone impose their own military techniques on you. Develop yours and fight for what you believe in, against all odds!

You will most likely meet someone new at this point who is all shiny and looks like he/she will be the right person to save you but that's just how the devil operates. The idiot knows that once you leave your man/woman to go to this shiny person, he has won by destroying something real and you'll soon realise that Mr/Miss Shiny is worse than your current partner.

I speak from experience when I tell you that when you fight the battle correctly and you patiently waited for the evil storm to blow over, that's when the real honeymoon phase sets in and this time it's forever.

It will never be a bed of roses, it will never be all sweet; but the proverbial phrase says, 'the patient dog eats the fattest bone'. I want that bone, don't you?